Gratia non tollit naturam

Books of Interest from St. Augustine's Press

David Walsh, *Person Means Relation*

D. C. Schindler, *God and the City: An Essay in Political Metaphysics*

Robert C. Koons, *Is St. Thomas's Aristotelian Philosophy of Nature Obsolete?*

Kevin Hart, *Contemplation and Kingdom: Aquinas Reads Richard of St. Victor*

Wayne J. Hankey, *Aquinas's Neoplatonism in the Summa Theologiae on God: A Short Introduction*

John F. Boyle, *Master Thomas Aquinas and the Fullness of Life*

Robert J. Spitzer, S.J., *Evidence for God from Physics and Philosophy*

Charles P. Nemeth, *Aquinas on Crime*

Charles P. Nemeth, *Christ, Crime, and Moral Judgment*

Peter Kreeft, *Summa Philosophica*

Peter Kreeft, *The Platonic Tradition*

St. Anselm of Canterbury (Matthew D. Walz, translator), *Proslogion*

Roberto Regoli, *Beyond the Crises in the Church: The Pontificate of Benedict XVI*

Gratia non tollit naturam

Technologies of the Self and the Catholic Constitution of Time and Space

Philipp W. Rosemann

St. Augustine's Press
South Bend, Indiana

Manufactured in the United States of America.

paperback ISBN: 978-1-58731-904-4
ebook ISBN: 978-1-58731-905-1

1 2 3 4 5 6 30 29 28 27 26 25

Library of Congress Control Number: 2025939480

For more information about the University of Dallas Aquinas Lectures, and a list of volumes available for purchase from St. Augustine's Press, see www.udallas.edu/aquinaslecture.

Table of Contents

NOTE

This volume is the fruit of the forty-second annual Aquinas Lecture at the University of Dallas, hosted by the Department of Philosophy and delivered by Philipp Rosemann, our former colleague, on January 29, 2024. We thank Dr. Rosemann once more for the opportunity think along with him, in the spirit of St. Thomas. We thank too our colleague Fr. James Lehrberger, for his formal response to the lecture and thoughtful introduction to this volume.

Thanks are due also to our colleague Cynthia Nielsen, for copy-editing the manuscripts, and to Benjamin Fingerhut of St. Augustine's Press, for his hard work and friendly professionalism.

Together with Dr. Rosemann, we dedicate this volume to Fr. James—our dear friend, and a true champion of the *verum, bonum, et pulchrum*—on the occasion of his retirement.

Faculty of the Department of Philosophy
University of Dallas
Feast of St. Adrian of Canterbury
January 9, 2025

Introduction: Despoiling the Postmodern Egyptian

James Lehrberger, OCist

Anyone who reads the book of Exodus knows the story of Moses and the Israelites despoiling the Egyptians during their flight out of Egypt. Hammered by the plagues, the Egyptian women willingly gave their gold and silver jewelry as well as their most beautiful clothes to the Israelites in order to hasten their departure from the land. Exodus also records the Israelites constructing the Sanctuary and adorning the Ark of the Covenant with that gold, silver, and precious cloth. In a very different but parallel case, Christian thinkers down through the ages have "despoiled" non-Christian philosophers of their insights and thinking in order to construct and adorn their understanding of the catholic and apostolic Faith. It suffices here to note just a few examples. St. Paul's Areopagus address to the Athenian Stoic and Epicurean philosophers appeals to Epimenides and Aratus to make known "the Unknown God" of Revelation. In the second and third centuries St. Justin Martyr, Clement of Alexandria, and Origen employed Platonic philosophy in order to defend and explain the Gospel. The fourth-century Council of Nicaea proclaimed that Jesus Christ was *homoousios* with the God the Father. Thinking derived from "the books of the Platonists" permeates St. Augustine's understanding and explanation of the Christian Faith. Later ages bear witness to this same theological despoiling of pagan philosophical thought. St. Thomas Aquinas famously used Aristotelian as well as Platonic categories in his vast synthesis of Christian theology. St. John Henry Newman learned from the empiricist John Locke in formulating his teaching on the assent of faith. In recent decades, Saints Edith Stein and John Paul II have incorporated significant elements of phenomenology into their accounts of *fides et ratio*. Bernard Lonergan's *Insight* relies on modern science for its Thomistic account of human understanding. Still, not all attempts to build the cathedral of faith with the aid of despoiled philosophical gold have been equally successful. Karl Rahner's use of Kant, Hegel, and Heidegger is questionable; even more problematic is Gustavo Gutierrez's adoption of Marx's categories to develop his "theology of liberation." Moreover, as the Egyptian gold that beautified the Sanctuary also provided the material for forging the golden calf, Platonic thought in many quarters also proved hostile to Christianity, and the Latin Averroists embraced an Aristotle who undermined the Catholic Faith. Can Michel Foucault's postmodernism do otherwise? Philipp Rosemann not only is convinced that a rich vein of gold runs through Foucault's thought, but has set himself the task of mining it in order to enrich the Faith.

At first glance, Michel Foucault's (1926–1984) philosophical reflections provide no obvious materials for Christian reflection.

Locating his own thought most broadly in the Kantian tradition and schooled by Nietzsche, Foucault was an atheist who denied the existence of human nature and of any metaphysical reality. Recognizing the temporal nature of human thought, he not only denied that there is any universal human reason, but asserted the purely historical and cultural character of all "reasoning"; and that is equally true of concepts such as "truth" and "liberty." His early membership in the French Communist Party and his later ambiguity on Marx reinforce this worry. His denial that any act is inherently just or unjust, right or wrong, pours fuel on the fire. He argues in many writings that the modern Western "self" is the product of historically contingent theories, political arrangements, and cultural practices; these subjugate us, leaving us with the illusion that we freely choose the person we wish to become. Most of his studies are thus "genealogical": they ultimately show that though modern man sees himself as a free self-constituting subject, his very subjectivity has become the object of reductionistic explanations in the human sciences, leaving little room for personal agency. Foucault's principal concern arises from this situation: discovering the way in which we can actively form ourselves rather than simply be victims of forces whose existence we do not even know. In a word, Foucault's concerns takes us back to the ancient problem of self-knowledge: know thyself!

Until the final years of his life, Foucault developed his philosophical genealogies almost exclusively in terms of modern analyses and practices; investigations of ancient philosophy and Christian thought were conspicuous by their almost complete absence. He initially turned his attention to ancient philosophy and early Christian thought only to uncover the genealogy of the modern self. While he did not abandon this purpose, during the course of his investigations he learned something new and unexpected: he discovered that "care of the self" and self-knowledge were major themes in these premodern thinkers. Thus, he came to see the necessity of studying them on their own terms. These thinkers look to the way that the self relates to itself, how it experiences itself. Working hand-in-glove with "care of the self" were the rather strict moral codes of the ancient philosophers: they realized that no one can govern a city who is unable to rule himself—and self-rule requires self-knowledge. The ancient philosophers, in short, were concerned with and undertook active self-formation. The early Christian thinkers largely accepted the moral code of the philosophers—with certain qualifications on sexual morality. (Even today, works like Aristotle's *Nicomachean Ethics* provide Christian thinkers with plenty of material for moral reflection.)

However, Foucault sharply distinguishes between "morality" and "ethics." While morality treats the laws and rules of behavior governing human acts in society, ethics looks to each individual in his relation to knowledge, power, and himself. In this realm an enormous difference between the ancient philosophers and the early Christian thinkers appears. More precisely, their "technologies of the self" differ quite radically. While the philosophers aim at the care of self to attain self-mastery for political rule or to live an otherwise "beautiful life," Christians examined and cared for themselves to attain union with God. The philosophers practiced truth-telling, *parrhesia,* to learn from their mistaken acts, while the Christians practiced *parrhesia* by telling the truth about their sins and inward struggles to their confessors or spiritual directors in order to direct their lives and thoughts solely to God. By these and other "technologies of the self"—ascetical fasts and abstinence, penances, personal and communal prayer, etc.—Christians shaped their own thoughts, desires, actions, choices, and speech in relation to God and thus their relations to others and to the world; and by these they formed themselves as moral agents. Foucault came to realize that he had overemphasized the role that the human sciences and "biopower" play in forming the self. It is interesting to speculate how the so-called "Christian turn" in Foucault's last writings would have played out had he lived long enough to complete these studies. Some even have speculated that he might have returned to the Catholic Faith, into which he was born.

If there is potential Christian gold to be discovered in Foucault's thought, Philipp Rosemann is the right prospector to find it. After earning his doctorate at Louvain University in Belgium, he began his teaching career at the then new Uganda Martyrs University. Moving to the University of Dallas, he taught for twenty years as a greatly appreciated and highly successful professor. Offered the prestigious Chair of Philosophy at Maynooth University in Ireland, he began teaching there in 2019. After several years at Maynooth, he accepted the University of Kentucky's offer to take up the Cottrill-Rolfes Chair of Catholic Studies. The author of eight books and almost ninety articles, Professor Rosemann's special interest lies in the intersection of medieval Christian thought and postmodern philosophy. His expertise in medieval Christian thought manifests itself in his books on Thomas Aquinas and Peter Lombard. Moreover, he is the founding editor of the greatly respected Dallas Library of Medieval Texts and Translations, a series of dual-language editions of often unedited and untranslated Latin texts.

His scholarship on Foucault and postmodernism is no less impressive. He has used Foucault as a lens through which to read scholastic thought, while his most recent book employs postmodern techniques to articulate a Catholic theory of tradition. Due to his outstanding scholarship, he was inducted into the Royal Irish Academy in 2020.

Unlike Foucault, who rejects metaphysics and natural philosophy out of hand, Professor Rosemann—as his two books on Aquinas's metaphysics make manifest—understands their necessity and importance. Far from sharing Foucault's atheism and rejection of Christianity, he wishes to serve man's knowledge of God and the truth of the Catholic Faith. While Foucault rejects metaphysics and human nature on claimed genealogical grounds, he should consider that the different opinions and accounts of such matters make the revival, perhaps in a new form, of the medieval "disputed questions" of ethics, metaphysics, and theology both possible and necessary, especially today. One can only wonder whether Foucault would have reconsidered his rejection had he lived long enough to study the great medieval doctors, above all St. Thomas Aquinas. In themselves, however, neither his genealogical methods nor his historical discoveries necessitate the rejection of metaphysics, much less the Catholic Faith. Distinguishing his historical analyses from his own philosophical presuppositions is a task needing to be undertaken. In any event, such considerations help explain Professor Rosemann's engagement with Foucault: he sympathetically and critically engages Foucault's thought and analyses in order to aid his own efforts to understand and advance the Gospel.

In a particular move that many will find surprising, Philipp Rosemann shows that key aspects of the thought of Joseph Ratzinger (later Pope Benedict XVI) can well be understood through Foucault's categories. Like Foucault, Ratzinger engages recent philosophers like Jürgen Habermas. He may even incorporate, directly or indirectly, certain elements of postmodern thought into his theology. Again like Foucault, Ratzinger has a strong interest in history. He even wrote his "habilitation" (a second doctoral dissertation required for teaching in a German university) on St. Bonaventure's theology of history. Unlike Foucault, however, he interprets history not as a collection of purely contingent facts and events but rather as events unfolding the Father's plan to restore all things in His Son. While Ratzinger published on many aspects of the Catholic Faith, he pays special attention to the Church's liturgy. In divine worship the God-man unites God and man, and the full dimensions of this unification are prayed and celebrated above all in the liturgy. As the reader of this volume will discover, Philipp Rosemann "despoils" Foucault's "technology of the self" by showing that Ratzinger's account of worship and prayer is a "technology" forming the Christian self. By this stunning analysis Philipp Rosemann has developed a powerful case that there is a rich vein of gold running through Foucault's postmodern thought that can and should be despoiled by Christian thinkers to build the sanctuary of faith to the glory to God.

I

Our Contemporary Predicament

Introduction: Gender Trouble

One of the most controversial issues of the day is whether it is possible for human beings to constitute who they are sexually through an act of performative speech. That is to say, if I were to stand in front of this audience and declare solemnly that I hitherto wished to be known and addressed as a woman, would this act, in fact, constitute me as a woman? There are, as we have all come to understand, two diametrically opposed answers to this question. For some, the act of performative speech—if it is exercised seriously and not in jest—is sufficient to change a person's gender. This is because gender is a social construct, and the sex assigned at birth cannot stand in the way of an individual's autonomous decision to determine who "they" are sexually. Such a decision must be respected unconditionally.

Against this position, others maintain that a person's sexual being is not a mere construct that can be changed at will. At birth, a newborn's sex is not "assigned," but rather diagnosed on the basis of anatomical features—at least in the vast majority of cases. Its sex is read off the body of the newborn, so to speak, not imposed upon it. Cases of gender dysphoria, where later in life a discrepancy arises between individuals' anatomical sex and their psychological sense of gender identity, are therefore deeply problematic. In particular, if these cases are becoming ever more numerous, as seems to be happening in the contemporary Western world, they cannot be resolved by sacrificing physical sexuality to psychological sense of gender. After all, as Scripture declares, "male and female he created them" (Gen. 1:27; cf. 5:2): sexuality is so profoundly inscribed into human nature that overriding it through autonomous decisions of persons who feel misgendered cannot become the norm. Some would therefore claim that acts of performative speech in which an individual announces a new gender are null and void.

In the opposing positions whose outlines I have attempted to sketch here,[1] several fundamental assumptions are at stake. One concerns the relationship between nature and culture or—to couch this in a more contemporary idiom—between reality and social construction. Is there a world that exists independently of how it is conceived and lived by its inhabi-

1 The argument is obviously more complex than the two preceding paragraphs are able to convey. The most authoritative statement of the traditional position is Pope John Paul II's book, *Man and Woman He Created Them: A Theology of the Body*, trans. Michael Waldstein (Boston: Pauline Books and Media, 2006). For a sympathetic account, from a Christian perspective, of sexual fluidity, one may refer to Scott Bader-Saye, "The Transgender Body's Grace," *Journal of the Society of Christian Ethics* 39:1 (2019): 75–92. I thank Dr. Cynthia Nielsen for this reference, as well as for incisive critical comments on my argument.

tants, or is reality subject to human constitution all the way down? It is difficult to deny that many aspects of human life are a matter of cultural performance; after all, Shakespeare already remarked, "All the world's a stage, And all the men and women merely players" (*As You Like It*, Act 2, Scene 7). As is well-known, the English word "person" is derived from the Latin *persona*, which originally designated a mask worn by actors.[2] But if the human world is a stage, is it nothing but a stage? Is there something behind the mask? To return to our earlier terminology, does culture build upon natural foundations, or does it supersede the latter entirely?

2 I should add here that this etymology is not uncontested, although it is itself of ancient origin. For an overview of current debates, see the well-documented piece by Helga María Lell, "Perspectiva histórica de la metáfora del concepto jurídico de persona. Etimología e ideas en la Antigüedad," *Díkaion: Revista de fundamentación jurídica* 28:2 (2019): 310–32. For a phenomenological interpretation of the significance of this etymology, one should read Chad Engelland, "Unmasking the Person," *International Philosophical Quarterly* 50:4 (2010): 447–60.

Much of our contemporary culture seems to have succumbed to a contradictory position in relation to these questions, maintaining, on the one hand, a strong version of biological determinism while, on the other, rejecting any limits placed upon the autonomy of the self-constituting subject. Thus, we are made to believe that race determines fundamentally and unchangeably who we are as persons, so that any attempt to self-constitute one's racial identity is greeted with outrage (think of cases where a white person has attempted to pass as Native American or Jewish[3]). Gender identity, by contrast, is taken to be so fluid, and so completely devoid of biological roots, that it can be changed through a simple act of performative speech. In a word, declaring, "I am Native American" does not make a white man Native American (even if he feels strong affinities to the Native American heritage); but saying, "I am a

3 There is even a word for someone falsely claiming Native American (or Canadian indigenous) heritage: a "pretendian." See the relevant entry in the Wikipedia, at https://en.wikipedia.org/wiki/Pretendian.

woman" immediately transforms him into a woman. This tension points to an instability in the set of fundamental assumptions—historical *a prioris*, Foucault would say—governing contemporary Western culture.

The conflict can also be couched in terms of the power of performative speech. Depending on where one stands in our unfortunate culture wars, the speech act "I am a woman," uttered by a man, is either "happy" or "unhappy," to use terminology suggested by J. L. Austin in his classic treatment of performatives, *How To Do Things With Words*.[4] Again, as already noted, few would consider the speech act "I am Native American," uttered by a white person, to be felicitous. So, then, what are the conditions that render performative speech acts successful? As Austin was the first to note, these speech acts are extremely important and widespread. Language intervenes in the order of reality all the time. "Doing things with

4 J. L. Austin, *How To Do Things With Words: The William James Lectures Delivered at Harvard University in 1955*, ed. J. O. Urmson and Marina Sbisà, 2nd ed. (Oxford: Oxford University Press, 1975).

words" is by no means unusual. Among many other possible examples, "I promise you . . ." constitutes a promise; "I order you . . ." is an act of ordering someone to do something; "I baptize you . . ." confers a name on an individual; and "I pronounce you husband and wife" legally creates a marital bond. In the Catholic context, the most important performative speech act undoubtedly is "This is my body . . . ," which—if spoken *in persona Christi*—effects the transubstantiation of a piece of bread into the Body of Christ. "I am a man," uttered by a woman, is not a totally different animal, at least structurally speaking.

How Did We Get Here?

But let us leave this controversy behind for the time being, to turn to the philosophical genealogy of our current predicament.[5] The first

5 I have offered a somewhat different—but complementary—genealogy in my essay, "How Did We Get Here? Reflections towards a Philosophy of the Present," *Studies: An Irish Quarterly Re-*

philosopher to maintain that there simply is no knowable world which is not a construct of the human mind was Immanuel Kant. In his *Prolegomena,* Kant famously wrote that "the understanding does not draw its (*a priori*) laws from nature, but prescribes them to it."[6] This claim turns the old scholastic principle according to which truth is *adaequatio rei et intellectus*[7] on its head: truth now no longer consists in a

view 110:439 (Autumn 2021): 279–91. The Irish essay focuses on the immanentization of the eschaton.

6 Kant, *Prolegomena to Any Future Metaphysics,* trans. Gary Hatfield, rev. ed., Cambridge Texts in the History of Philosophy (Cambridge: Cambridge University Press, 2004), §36, pp. 73–4 (= Ak 4:320). This sentence is highlighted in the original text, to emphasize its significance.—What exactly is an *a priori* law? How much of the laws of nature derive from *a priori* constitution rather than experience? Michael Friedman examines the case of the law of gravitation, which Kant offers as an example in §38, in "Kant on Space, the Understanding, and the Law of Gravitation: *Prolegomena* §38," *The Monist* 72:2 (1989): 236–84.

7 One of the central places where this principle is cited in Aquinas is *ST* I, qu. 16, art. 1.

conformity of the (human) intellect to the things that it apprehends but, inversely, in the conformity of the things to the *a priori* laws of the intellect. In positing his Copernican revolution, Kant in fact assigned the human mind a function not entirely unlike the constitutive, creative role that premodern metaphysics found only in God. For, the principle *veritas est adaequatio rei et intellectus* can mean either of two things: that truth stems from the human mind's success in bringing itself into alignment with the state of affairs it attempts to apprehend, or that the created order reflects the truth of the divine Mind from whom it originated.[8]

8 Here one can cite the classical text of Thomas Aquinas, *De veritate*, qu. 1, art. 2c: "Res ergo naturalis inter duos intellectus constituta, secundum adaequationem ad utrumque vera dicitur; secundum enim adaequationem ad intellectum divinum dicitur vera, in quantum implet hoc ad quod est ordinata per intellectum divinum . . . ; secundum autem adaequationem ad intellectum dicitur res vera, in quantum est nata de se facere veram aestimationem; . . . Prima autem ratio veritatis per prius inest rei quam secunda, quia prius est eius comparatio ad intellectum divinum quam humanum."

Kantian philosophy, then, can be read as a divinization of the human intellect.[9]

The *Critique of Pure Reason* impressively spells out the consequences of this new conception of truth in terms of man's relationship to the natural world:

> [Galileo, Torricelli, and Stahl] learned that reason has insight only into that which it produces after a plan of its own, and that it must not allow itself to be kept, as it were, in nature's leading-strings, but must itself show the way with principles of judgment based upon fixed laws, constraining

9 One could equally say that, in Thomistic terms, Kant conceives of the speculative intellect along the lines of the practical one. Once natural beings come to be conflated with artefacts, the human intellect becomes the measure of things. Consider this excerpt from the *De veritate*: "Intellectus enim practicus causat res, unde est mensura rerum quae per ipsum fiunt: sed intellectus speculativus, quia accipit a rebus, est quodam modo motus ab ipsis rebus, et ita res mensurant ipsum" (*De veritate*, qu. 1, art. 2c).

> [*nötigen*] nature to give answer to questions of reason's own determining. . . . Reason, holding in one hand its principles, according to which alone concordant appearances can be admitted as equivalent to laws, and in the other hand the experiment which it has devised in conformity with these principles, must approach nature in order to be taught by it. It must not, however, do so in the character of a pupil who listens to everything that the teacher chooses to say, but of an appointed judge who compels [*nötigen*] the witnesses to answer questions which he has himself formulated.[10]

"It is thus," concludes Kant, "that the study of nature has entered on the secure path of a science, after having for so many centuries

10 Kant, *Critique of Pure Reason,* trans. Norman Kemp Smith (London: Macmillan, 1929), Preface to the Second Edition, 20 (B xiii–xiv).

been nothing but a process of merely random groping."[11]

Let me highlight two critical points in this quotation. First, we note the language of compulsion that Kant employs in describing man's relationship to nature. Our role is not to contemplate nature like docile pupils but to put it on the witness stand to answer our questions. The German verb which, in the passage quoted above, is rendered as "constraining" and "compelling," *nötigen,* has connotations so violent that the word could be employed to describe rape.[12] The German-speaking countries still regard *Nötigung*—the use of an overwhelming physical or psychological force to compel the will of another—as a crime.[13] In his

11 Ibid., 20–1 (B xiv).

12 In their *Deutsches Wörterbuch,* the Grimm brothers paraphrase the expression *sie nötigen die weiber* as *zwingen sie zum beischlaf,* that is, "they force the women into intercourse" (Jacob and Wilhelm Grimm, *Deutsches Wörterbuch,* 16 vols. [Leipzig: Hirzel, 1854–1961], vol. 13, col. 942).

13 In Germany, *Nötigung* is dealt with in §240 of the *Strafgesetzbuch;* the corresponding Austrian law is §105; in Switzerland it is article 181.

use of such a problematic term to describe scientific experimentation, Kant followed the example of Francis Bacon, one of the first theoreticians of the modern scientific method, who regularly drew upon violent metaphors to convey his conception of the controlled experiment.[14]

The second point to note concerns the motivation for Kant's radical reinterpretation of the *adaequatio rei et intellectus*: it is to render philosophy scientific, after millennia of what the philosopher from Königsberg regards as fruitless disagreements—"random groping" instead of steady growth in the discovery of truth. How exactly Kant gets from his admiration of modern scientific progress to transcendental idealism is not something we need to reconstruct here in detail. In essence, Kant believes that, just as the laws of logic and mathematics owe their unshakeable

14 On Bacon's use of violent metaphors, one may read the excellent piece by Caroline Merchant, "'The Violence of Impediments': Francis Bacon and the Origins of Experimentation," *Isis* 99:4 (2008): 731–60.

validity to the fact that they rely on no sense experience, so only the turn to the fundamental laws of the mind itself, independent of all sensory input, can ensure a sound basis for metaphysical inquiry. In this manner, metaphysics for Kant becomes epistemology, that is to say, investigation of the *a priori* conditions for the possibility of experience.

One can certainly lament this transformation and criticize transcendental idealism from any number of angles. At one level, however, Kant's reversal of the meaning of the *adaequatio rei et intellectus* is difficult to challenge—namely, not as theory but as a description of life in the modern age. It has become increasingly hard, due to technological developments stretching at least as far back as the First Industrial Revolution, to recognize the structures of nature in our daily living. It is especially the technological infrastructure of the industrialized world which at once makes human life so much more comfortable than in the past, and imposes itself upon natural forms in such a manner as to utterly conceal man's embeddedness in, and indebtedness to them. Indeed, humanity's goal seems to be to emancipate itself from nature as far as possible—to absorb nature entirely into culture. Kant himself considered it "the ultimate goal of the moral vocation of the human species" that "perfect art again becomes nature."[15] To frame this goal in terms of the inversion of another scholastic principle, for Kant humanity will overcome the alienating consequences of the Fall[16] only once *natura imitatur artem*. We have not yet quite reached the state where nature has been completely subdued in the torture rack of experimentation and the structures of human "art," but—we are

15 Kant, "Conjectural Beginning of Human History," in Kant, *Anthropology, History, and Education*, ed. Günter Zöller and Robert B. Louden, The Cambridge Edition of the Works of Immanuel Kant (Cambridge: Cambridge University Press, 2007), 163–75, at 171. The *Akademie-Ausgabe* (Ak 8:117–18) reads: "bis vollkommene Kunst wieder Natur wird: als welches das letzte Ziel der sittlichen Bestimmung der Menschengattung ist."

16 For this is the context of the remark just cited from "Conjectural Beginning of Human History."

coming closer.[17] Only consider the dystopian vision of human life that transhumanism espouses.[18]

Kant would have been horrified at the notion that the transcendental structures which he uncovered in the *Critique of Pure Reason* could be subject to change. He firmly held to the belief that transcendental idealism was by no means a form of subjectivism or relativism; on the contrary, he regarded it

17 Hans Blumenberg offers a much more positive interpretation of the modern challenge to the principle *ars imitatur naturam*, a challenge that according to him goes back as far as Nicholas of Cusa and even has a distant precursor in Thomas Aquinas. See Blumenberg, "'Imitation of Nature': Toward a Prehistory of the Idea of the Creative Being," trans. Anna Wertz, in *History, Metaphors, Fables: A Hans Blumenberg Reader*, ed. Hannes Bajohr, Florian Fuchs, and Joe Paul Kroll (Ithaca, NY: Cornell University Press, 2020), 316–57.

18 Or gender ideology, which subjects sexuality to human "art." On this subject, see the excellent article by Michele Schumacher, "Gender Ideology and the 'Artistic' Fabrication of Human Sex: Nature as Norm or the Remaking of the Human?" *The Thomist* 80:3 (2016): 363–43.

as securely anchoring the objectivity of knowledge. For Kant, there is no plurality of *a priori* frames in and through which human experience is possible.

The nineteenth century, however, discovered history as the ultimate *a priori*. All human experience—indeed, all being—is related to time not in a merely accidental fashion, as Aristotle believed, but in such a way that historical process constitutes the ultimate horizon in which reality takes shape. Thus, in the nineteenth century history emerged for the first time as an academic discipline, not only with its own objectivity and method but with the aspiration of understanding all aspects of human reality. While the theoreticians of modern historical method—scholars like Leopold von Ranke and Wilhelm Dilthey—carefully distinguished between the humanities (*Geisteswissenschaften,* literally "sciences of the spirit") and the natural sciences, Darwin argued that even nature is historical, for biological species evolve over time. The subsumption of all reality under history culminated in Hegel, who discovered that being itself is not static, given once and for all, but unfolds over the course of history toward its full realization. Hegel's theory of substance becoming subject pulls even God into historical process, but—unlike Darwin's evolution of species—this process is strictly teleological, following a stringent logic and leading to nothing less than the end of history. Hegel's history is rational, driven by Reason and Spirit, not by chance, accident, or power.

Nietzsche, preceded by Schopenhauer, is the last major step that we have to understand in order to appreciate the main forces at work in our own cultural situation. Nietzsche too is a historian of reason, very "nineteenth-century" in this regard. But his version of history is not of the same kind as the Hegelian account of the triumphant march of Reason through time toward self-transparency and freedom. It is the opposite: a genealogy of the decline of (Western) reason after its flowering in pre-Socratic Greece, where tragedy was born out of the Dionysian spirit of music. The decline is due to Judaism and Christianity, to the will to power of small-minded losers and their resentment. Whereas the Greeks worshipped heroes, Jews indulge in stories of exile and persecution while Christians believe in a savior who died, humiliated and tortured, like a slave. Fortunately, according to Nietzsche, the myth of God that these losers invented to help them to power is dead now, so that we have the opportunity for a new beginning. The Overman has the chance to create new, better values, overcoming the nihilism of post-Christian culture through the sheer force of imagination and creativeness.

All this is a mix as brilliant as it is explosive. With Nietzsche begins the deconstruction of Western reason, the effort to show that its grand edifices are built on pettiness and power. The theories it has invented are elaborate metaphors—lies—and its values are in reality countervalues.[19] Everything is merely appearance; the ultimate foundations

19 See, respectively, "On Truth and Lies in a Nonmoral Sense" (1873) and *On the Genealogy of Morals* (1887).

that metaphysics purports to have established are also nothing but fictions. Everything therefore is surface, myth, performance—with the important proviso that some myths are better than others for genuine human flourishing. *Thus Spake Zarathustra* is Nietzsche's attempt to create such a myth.

The twentieth century attempted to synthesize Kant's transcendental idealism with the historicism of the nineteenth century. The Neo-Kantian movement provides an example of a first attempt of such a synthesis, most notably perhaps in the thought of Ernst Cassirer. For Cassirer, human beings encounter reality through a number of symbolization processes—the "symbolic forms" of language, myth, religion, science, and art—that bestow order upon the raw material of sense data. We are dealing here with a multiplicity of *a prioris,* but their relationship to history remains vague. While myth, for instance, would seem to belong to an earlier stage than science in the development of the human being as *animal symbolicum,* Cassirer refrains from the Hegelian conclusion that consciousness evolves from lower to higher forms.[20]

Heidegger grappled with the same challenge of synthesizing the principles of the *Critique of Pure Reason* with the legacy of nineteenth-century historicism. *Being and Time* bears the hallmarks of this struggle, as Heidegger endeavored to articulate his fundamentally historical account not only of human being, but indeed of Being itself, through the categories of transcendental idealism. However, he quickly came to understand the limitations of this approach for his project of recovering the question of Being. Dasein is not a transcendental subject who constitutes the world, but is always already in the world, which it encounters within the horizon of time. In the later Heidegger's thought, therefore, history—or, rather, *das Geschick*, the "sending" of Being in time—assumed an uneasy transcendental

20 For a sophisticated introduction to the philosophy of symbolic forms, see Steve G. Lofts, *Cassirer: A "Repetition" of Modernity*, SUNY Series in Contemporary Philosophy (Albany, NY: State University of New York Press, 2000).

function.[21] Whether Heidegger ever succeeded in leaving Kant behind is an ongoing debate.[22]

Foucault: From the "Empirico-Transcendental Doublet" to Technologies of the Self

In some ways, the most impressive synthesis of transcendental idealism with historicism may be the philosophy of Michel Foucault. In the 1960s and early 1970s, the attempt to think the *a priori* historically constituted the methodological center of his work. In the *Archaeology of Knowledge*, Foucault even coined the term "historical *a priori*," fully aware that

21 I have argued this point in "Heidegger's Transcendental History," *Journal of the History of Philosophy* 40:4 (2002): 501–23.

22 Chad Engelland argues that he did not; see *Heidegger's Shadow: Kant, Husserl, and the Transcendental Turn* (New York and London: Routledge, 2017).

within the framework of strict Kantianism this "rather barbarous term"—as he said—made no sense at all. He continued:

> This *a priori* does not elude historicity: it does not constitute, above events, and in an unmoving heaven, an atemporal structure; it is defined as the totality of rules that characterize a discursive practice: but these rules are not imposed from the outside on the elements that they relate together; they are caught up in the very things that they connect.[23]

This *a priori*, Foucault is saying, does not belong to a transcendental subject but names the rules that make possible a certain "discursive practice." What are the conditions for the possibility of people thinking and acting

23 Foucault, *The Archaeology of Knowledge and The Discourse on Language*, trans. A. M. Sheridan Smith (New York: Pantheon Books, 1972), 127. I have amended the translation in light of the French text: *L'archéologie du savoir*, Bibliothèque des sciences humaines (Paris: Gallimard, 1969), 168.

in a certain way at a particular point in history?—that is the question which the historical *a priori* is meant to answer. Again, in Foucault's own words:

> In a society, different bodies of learning, philosophical ideas, everyday opinions, but also institutions, commercial practices and police activities, mores—all refer to a certain implicit knowledge [*savoir*] special to this society. This knowledge is profoundly different from the bodies of learning [*des connaissances*] that one can find in scientific books, philosophical theories, and religious justifications, but it is what makes possible at a given moment the appearance of a theory, an opinion, a practice.[24]

24 Foucault, "The Order of Things" (trans. J. Johnston), in: *Essential Works of Foucault 1954–1984*, ed. Paul Rabinow, vol. 2: *Aesthetics, Method, and Epistemology* (New York: The Free Press, 1998), 261–7, at 261. The bracketed terms are included in the translation.

One of the fruits of Foucault's research on this "implicit knowledge," and the question of how it changes over time, was his book translated—or should one say mistranslated—as *The Order of Things*. The French title was different, more aptly reflecting the content of the work: *Les mots et les choses*, "Words and Things." In *Words and Things*, Foucault set out to conduct what he called "archaeological" research to unearth the hidden strata beneath the modern understanding of what constitutes knowledge, specifically in the areas of life (biology), labor (economics), and language (linguistics). The story Foucault tells in this book is one of a gradual drifting apart of words and things, which in the premodern era still formed a whole: the "prose of the world," as the title of chapter 2 puts it. Up until the Renaissance, the world itself was a text to be deciphered, so that the question of how words and things were related could not arise. In the modern age, after world and language drifted apart, the transcendental subject holds the world together. At the same time, however, this subject comes to be *subject to* empirical research in biology and the social sciences, and that research demonstrates its radical finitude. There is no transcendental subject, from this point of view, only a subject constituted by a myriad of biological, social, and historical factors. Foucault calls this paradox the "empirico-transcendental doublet" or "empirico-transcendental reduplication."[25] He regards it as the fundamental crux of the modern project, the point that renders it unstable at its very core. We believe in a constitutive subject that we keep deconstructing. This cannot work. We have seen this in our initial consideration of the "gender trouble"[26] that affects contemporary society. On the one

25 Foucault, *The Order of Things: An Archaeology of the Human Sciences* [no translator given] (New York: Vintage Books, 1994), 319 and 336, respectively. The French terms are *doublet empirico-transcendantal* and *redoublement empirico-transcendantal* (*Les mots et les choses. Une archéologie des sciences humaines,* Collection Tel [Paris: Gallimard, 1966], 330 and 347, respectively).

26 "Gender trouble" is of course the title of Judith Butler's influential book, *Gender Trouble: Feminism and the Subversion of Identity* (London and New York: Routledge, 1990).

hand, as gendered, persons function as Kantian-type subjects, endowed with sovereign authority to constitute their own sexuality. Yet on the other hand, as belonging to a particular race, these same subjects are confronted with the radical finitude of being "thrown," as Heidegger would say, into a world not of their own making.

And the solution to the paradoxes of the empirico-transcendental doublet? In *Words and Things,* Foucault ventures the suggestion that language—in particular the relationship between the human being and language—must become central once again in philosophical inquiry:

> Is the task ahead of us to advance toward a mode of thought, unknown hitherto in our culture, that would make it possible to reflect at the same time, without discontinuity or contradiction, the being of man and the being of language?[27]

27 Foucault, *The Order of Things,* 338. Translation amended in light of the French text: "Est-ce que

Why language? Because language is the carrier of the "discursive practices" that shape the subject. But then the being of this subject, too, needs to be given its due weight, so that being constitut*ed* and constitut*ing* can be reflected upon in their dialectical entanglement.

Foucault is well-known for the ruptures in this oeuvre, the deliberate new turns that his thinking takes in each of his books. (In fact, he devoted a humorous fictional dialogue to this situation in the final pages of the *Archaeology of Knowledge*.) There is therefore no explicit line connecting the remark just quoted—which Foucault never repeats, as far as I know—with his subsequent intellectual endeavors. Nevertheless, as we shall see shortly, in the last years of his life, Foucault attempted to carve out a space for subjective agency within the very discursive

notre tâche à venir est de nous avancer vers un mode de pensée, inconnu jusqu'à présent dans notre culture, et qui permettrait de réfléchir à la fois, sans discontinuité ni contradiction, l'être de l'homme et l'être du langage?" (*Les mots et les choses*, 349).

practices in which the subject is necessarily implicated.

So we turn to Foucault's final *magnum opus*, the *History of Sexuality* in four volumes, the last of which was published posthumously, indeed thirty-four years after its author's death.[28] Again, Foucault sets out to understand contemporary structures of thinking and living by showing that the unarticulated presuppositions which undergird them are historically contingent: an *a priori* that "does not elude historicity." This type of research is meant to create a space for freedom, by demonstrating that what we consider to be normal is in fact just one possible discursive practice among others. However, the kind of sexual liberation at which Foucault aims in the *History of Sexuality* is paradoxical: in fact, he wants to liberate us from sexual liberation itself, which—he

28 For a critical perspective on the posthumous publication of volume four, it is worth reading Mark D. Jordan, "In Search of Foucault's Last Words," *Boston Review* (January 19, 2022), https://www.bostonreview.net/articles/in-search-of-foucaults-last-words/.

claims—is a myth. The story usually told about the emergence of contemporary sexuality—namely, as a progressive overcoming of Victorian repression—needs fundamental revision. There has been no liberation, but something quite different: a harnessing of sex by discourse. We cannot stop talking about sex, in all its various, continuously proliferating forms.

Now Foucault makes a couple of moves that are as surprising as they are controversial. First, he argues that the contemporary way of "transforming sex into discourse"[29] and thus "normalizing" it—bringing it under norms, making it governable—represents a strategy of "biopolitics." Modern governments rule biopolitically by bringing power to bear directly on life itself.[30]

29 Foucault, *The History of Sexuality*, vol. 1: *An Introduction*, trans. Robert Hurley (New York: Vintage Books, 1990), 22.

30 This is a vast topic. For a first introduction, one may wish to consult Thomas Lemke, *Biopolitics: An Advanced Introduction*, trans. Eric Frederick Trump (New York and London: New York University Press, 2011).

Secondly, a central tool of this biopolitical rule is a modern transformation of an old Christian practice of governing the self: confession. Western man is a "confessing animal,"[31] but instead of talking about our sins to a confessor in the hope of redemption, we now talk about our sexual thoughts and actions in medical or psychological terms, in painstaking detail, and frequently even in public.

This is the strange beginning of Foucault's journey into Christian sources, which played no role in his earlier research, where usually the Renaissance formed a quickly sketched backdrop for inquiries concerning the modern age. The *History of Sexuality*, by contrast, delves deeply both into pagan antiquity and the writings of the Church Fathers, the latter with such verve that Foucault scholars have begun to speak of a "Christian turn" in his work.[32] The final

31 Foucault, *History of Sexuality*, vol. 1, 59.

32 I provide a review of some recent French research in "On the 'Christian Turn' in Foucault's Thought: Apropos of *Foucault, les Pères, le sexe*," *Maynooth Philosophical Papers* 11 (2022): 75–84.

volume, the posthumous one, surprises readers with detailed interpretations of patristic texts on marriage and virginity. But Foucault was not interested in Christian treatments of sexuality for their moral lessons; his focus was different. He was fascinated by what, already in the title of volume 3, devoted to pagan antiquity, he called "care of the self." How is it that, through particular attention to the details of bodily existence, and indeed a certain austerity in its regard—mistrust of pleasure, especially—the Greeks and Romans of the imperial period developed an "art of living under the theme of the care of oneself"?[33]

Foucault himself considered his new focus on the "care of the self" a corrective in relation to his earlier emphasis on overarching structures. In a seminar that he taught at the University of Vermont in 1982, he admitted, "Perhaps I've insisted too much on the technology of domination and power. I am more and more interested in the interaction

33 Foucault, *The History of Sexuality*, vol. 3: *The Care of the Self*, trans. Robert Hurley (New York: Vintage Books, 1988), 45.

between oneself and others and in the technologies of individual domination, the history of how an individual acts upon himself, in the technology of self."[34] More concretely, these technologies

> permit individuals to effect by their own means or with the help of others a certain number of operations on their own bodies and souls, thoughts, conduct, and way of being, so as to transform themselves in order to attain a certain state of happiness, purity, wisdom, perfection, or immortality.[35]

34 *Technologies of the Self: A Seminar with Michel Foucault*, ed. Luther H. Martin, Huck Gutman, and Patrick H. Hutton (Amherst: University of Massachusetts Press, 1988), 19. This text represents a transcript of Foucault's seminar which he did not have an opportunity to review before his death.

35 Ibid., 18. Foucault had a habit of providing (frequently shifting) interpretations of the logic behind his own oeuvre. At the University of Vermont, he presented the following schema: "through studying madness and psychiatry,

Lessons from Foucault for Catholic Thought

If we approach Foucault's thought as a reflection both of and upon the current state of Western philosophy—that is to say, at once a product of that philosophy and an attempt to address its aporias—then what lessons can we draw from his intellectual itinerary, specifically for Catholic thought? Synthesizing two dominant philosophical trends since Kant—transcendental idealism and historicism—Foucault applies his method to a series of pressing social and political issues, from the treatment of mental illness and the dissemination and solidification of formerly marginal sexualities to the rise of biopolitics.

crime and punishment, I have tried to show how we have indirectly constituted ourselves through the exclusion of some others: criminals, mad people, and so on. And now my present work deals with the question: How did we directly constitute our identity through some ethical techniques of the self which developed through antiquity down to now?" (ibid., 146).

In the end, as Pierre Hadot has noted, he rediscovers the ancient tradition of philosophy understood not merely as an attempt to explain the world, but as a way of life.[36] What matters to Foucault, in the end, is a concern with "a certain state of happiness, purity, wisdom, perfection, or immortality." He conceives of the subject as being at one and the same time a product of "technologies of power, which determine the conduct of individuals and submit them to certain ends or domination, an objectivizing of the subject,"[37] *and* able to deploy techniques, strategies to shape the self autonomously. Foucault coins the term "governmentality" to encompass both aspects.[38]

36 Pierre Hadot, *Philosophy as a Way of Life: Spiritual Exercises from Socrates to Foucault* (Oxford: Blackwell, 1995). Also see the more recent study by Edward F. McGushin, *Foucault's Askesis: An Introduction to the Philosophical Life* (Evanston, IL: Northwestern University Press, 2007).

37 Foucault, *Technologies of the Self*, 18.

38 Ibid., 19: "This contact between the technologies of domination of others and those of the self I call governmentality."

But, again, what insight can Catholic thought derive from this? The insight, it seems to me, that it remains possible to shape a Catholic self even while that self is implicated in social structures which run counter to—even fundamentally undermine—a Christian form of existence. For that is the challenge we are facing: to survive and, indeed, flourish as Christians in a world whose structures stand in direct conflict with the Christian conception not only of the good life but of reality itself.[39] While this challenge shocks us, after almost two thousand years in which many elements of Christianity could be taken for granted in the Western approach to the world, it is by no means

39 The realization of the existence of this conflict was the impetus behind Rod Dreher's much-discussed book, *The Benedict Option: A Strategy for Christians in a Post-Christian Nation* (New York: Sentinel, 2017). Ironically, Alasdair MacIntyre, from whom Dreher derived the concept of the "Benedict option," has been highly critical of Dreher's approach. See "'A New Set of Social Forms': Alasdair MacIntyre on the 'Benedict Option,'" *Tradistae* (21 April 2020), https://tradistae.com/2020/04/21/macintyre-benop/.

unprecedented. The Christian faith came into existence, after all, as the result of a series of radical transgressions of intellectual and religious norms.[40] God shattered both Jewish and pagan horizons of expectation as to who he is, and what he can do. In the cultural context in which it originated, faith in Jesus Christ was a scandal to the Jews, and an absurdity to the Gentiles: "we preach Christ crucified, unto the Jews a stumbling block, and unto the Greeks foolishness," St. Paul declared (1 Cor. 1:23).[41] So, back to the origins! The challenge of forming Christian selves in adverse cultural circumstances has deep roots in the Church. She possesses all the spiritual resources necessary to this end. In what follows, I discuss these resources

40 A theme I explore in greater depth in my book, *Charred Root of Meaning: Continuity, Transgression, and the Other in Christian Tradition*, Interventions (Grand Rapids, MI: Eerdmans, 2018).

41 Σκάνδαλον and μωρίαν are the respective Greek terms for "stumbling block" and "foolishness." Unless otherwise noted, quotations of Scripture are from the Douay-Rheims translation.

within a contemporary theoretical frame, with the goal of highlighting their relevance in the constellation of philosophical ideas that marks our own time. For that purpose, as I have tried to explain in the preceding sections, the Foucauldian notion of "technologies of the self" is particularly apt.

An Objection

But there is an obvious objection to this approach. Foucault's concept of "technologies of the self" belongs in the context of a modern philosophical project that is ultimately Kantian: namely, to liberate the self from oppressive structures of power that prevent it from acting autonomously. Indeed, one of the last pieces of work Foucault was able to complete before he died was an essay asking Kant's very question, "What is Enlightenment?" Furthermore, for a notoriously elusive thinker who detested labels, Foucault was remarkably forthcoming in declaring his allegiance to Kant's way of thinking: "To the extent that Foucault fits into the philosophical tradition," the philosopher wrote about himself in an entry for a French encyclopedia, "it is the *critical* tradition of Kant."[42] But the goal of Christian life clearly is not enlightenment in the Kantian sense—how could it be if the light that we are ultimately seeking is not the light of our own reason but the "light from light" who is God himself! Therefore, any "technology of the self" inspired by the Kantian project runs completely counter to Christian living and thinking.

There is a twofold answer to this concern. The first answer is that, in the essay "What is Enlightenment?"—as well as two others devoted to the same subject—Foucault articulates a very nuanced stance toward the Enlightenment project. Rather than simply restating Kantian positions, he reinterprets them in the context of his own philosophical itinerary and ethos. But

42 Maurice Florence, "Foucault," trans. Robert Hurley, in *Essential Works of Foucault*, vol. 2, 459–63, at 459. Emphasis in the original. "Maurice Florence" is the pseudonym Foucault chose when he composed the entry on himself for the *Dictionnaire des philosophes*.

one of the major impulses animating Foucault's philosophy is the rejection of the normalizing forces that he sees at work in modernity, that is to say, the extension of a finely woven network of governance to all areas of society to ensure the rule of "reason" and scientific progress. Against such normalization, Foucault affirms, in the words of M. P. d'Entrèves, an "ethos of transgression and aesthetic self-fashioning . . . much closer to Nietzsche's vision of a transvaluation of values than to Kant's notion of maturity."[43] One may wonder whether it is not precisely such an "ethos of transgression and aesthetic self-fashioning" that is needed in the Christian response to secular society and the reduced vision of reason and the good life which it embodies.[44]

43 Maurizio Passerin d'Entrèves, "Between Nietzsche and Kant: Michel Foucault's Reading of 'What is Enlightenment?'," *History of Political Thought* 20:2 (1999): 337–56, at 356.

44 A lot has been written about the possibility (or not) of a Christian appropriation of Nietzsche. A classic treatment is Eugen Biser, *"Gott ist tot."*

This leads us to a second point. The late Foucault's "Christian turn" allowed him to understand that the goal of any authentically Christian technology of the self could not be the formation of a Kantian subject. Rather, his study of ancient practices of confession led him to the conclusion that the Christian self is one discovering within itself the abyss of sin in light of the Truth, who is the Word. Foucault recognized that these two aspects are indissociable, forming the two sides of the idea of confession. In a set of notes for the

Nietzsches Destruktion des christlichen Bewußtseins (Munich: Kösel, 1962). James Lehrberger O.Cist. ("'The Blessed in the Kingdom of Heaven Will See the Punishments of the Damned So That Their Bliss May Be More Delightful to Them': Nietzsche and Aquinas," *The Thomist* 80:3 [2016]: 425–62) argues that Nietzsche and Aquinas have more in common than might appear on the face of it. In particular, Nietzsche "eagerly desires to recover human flourishing, nobility, and excellence" (461). Lehrberger concludes: "Nietzsche's noble morality resonates much more closely with Aquinas's natural law, virtue, and Christian ethic than he realizes" (462).

fourth volume of the *History of Sexuality*, he explained:

> Truth-telling and believing, veridiction in regard to oneself and faith in the Word, are or should be inseparable. The duty of truth, as belief and as confession, is at the center of Christianity. The two traditional meanings of the word "confession" include these two aspects. In a general way, "confession" is the recognition of the duty of truth.[45]

Through his study of the Fathers of the Church, the late Foucault began to appreciate the fundamental logic of the Christian self: it has to die to itself in order to attain the fullness of freedom. It is a self that needs to

45 Foucault, *Confessions of the Flesh: The History of Sexuality, volume 4*, trans. Robert Hurley (London: Penguin, 2021), Appendix 3, p. 320. I have moved a comma to reflect the sense of the French text, for which see *Les aveux de la chair*, ed. Frédéric Gros, Bibliothèque des histoires (Paris: Gallimard, 2018), 402.

break with its attachment to the world and discover, within itself, a deeper dimension that only God's grace renders accessible.[46]

46 I am paraphrasing Arianna Sforzini's incisive interpretation of Foucault's lectures *On the Government of the Living*, in her article, "Brève généalogie des *Aveux de la chair*, 1977–1984," in *Foucault, les Pères, le sexe. Autour des "Aveux de la chair,"* ed. Philippe Büttgen et al., La philosophie à l'œuvre 28 (Paris: Éditions de la Sorbonne, 2021), 19–36, esp. 34.

II

Christian Technologies of the Self

The "Liturgical Subject"

For Foucault, as we have seen, the paradigmatic Christian technology of the self was confession. Foucault focused on confession because he attempted to uncover the premodern roots of the "confessing animal" that Western man has become. When, toward the end of his life, he delved more deeply into the Christian tradition itself, he broadened his inquiry to include the "arts of virginity" and marriage.[47] But what about other

47 In the fourth volume of the *History of Sexuality*, Part II is entitled "Being Virgin," and Part III carries the title "Being Married."

technologies of the self Christians have employed to shape who they are? No doubt there are many, from personal prayer and popular devotions to the practice of charity. The liturgy, however, stands out: it is central since it is the worship of the Church as a whole, as Body of Christ. Indeed, it is in the celebration of the Eucharist that the Body of Christ is formed: in the famous words of Henri de Lubac, it is not only that the Church in some sense "makes" the Eucharist, but the Eucharist itself also makes the Church.[48] Any consideration of Christian technologies of the self will therefore have to start with the liturgy. In recognition of this fact, recent scholarship has coined the term "liturgical subject" to designate the kind of self that takes shape in liturgical celebration.[49]

48 The famous formula first occurs in *Corpus mysticum*: "L'Église et l'Eucharistie se font, chaque jour, l'une par l'autre" (*Corpus mysticum. L'Eucharistie et l'Église au moyen âge. Étude historique*, 2nd ed. [Paris: Aubier, 1949], 292).

49 As it happens, two recent volumes carry "liturgical subject" in their titles: *Liturgical Subject: Subject, Subjectivity, and the Human Person in*

The Liturgy and Speech that Is Action

So, then, what is liturgy? In an important sense, liturgy is nothing but Christian life itself, thought from its end. Liturgy is not simply a set of words spoken and gestures enacted when one happens to be at Mass—but it is, again, all of life, considered teleologically. This is the position of William Durand of Mende, celebrated author of the thirteenth-century *Rationale divinorum officiorum*, an encyclopedic interpretation of the

Contemporary Liturgical Discussion and Critique, ed. James G. Leachman OSB (Notre Dame: Notre Dame University Press, 2009), and Derek Krueger, *Liturgical Subjects: Christian Ritual, Biblical Narrative, and the Formation of the Self in Byzantium* (University Park, PA: University of Pennsylvania Press, 2014). The term is used in French scholarship as well; so, for example, François Cassingena-Trévedy OSB speaks of "sujet liturgique" in his study *Les Pères de l'Église et la liturgie. Un esprit, une expérience. De Constantin à Justinien* (Paris: Desclée de Brouwer, 2009).

liturgical rites of the Church. In the heavenly Jerusalem, William notes, there will be unending song and praise, day and night: "And they rested not day and night, saying: Holy, holy, holy, Lord God Almighty" (Apoc. 4:8). Having quoted this verse, William distinguishes the Church triumphant of the heavenly Jerusalem from the Church militant that exists in this life. He explains, "the Church militant cannot fully imitate the Church triumphant because . . . we are unable, with the shackles of our infirmity, to persevere continually in the divine praises at each of the twelve hours of the day." This is due to the fact that, sadly, "man by necessity sometimes has to give attention to the needs of the body."[50]

50 William Durand, *Rationale, Book Five: Commentary on the Divine Office,* trans. Timothy M. Thibodeau, Corpus Christianorum in Translation 23 (Turnhout: Brepols, 2015), 63–4. The Latin text is Guillelmi Duranti *Rationale divinorum officiorum V–VI,* ed. A. Davril OSB and T. M. Thibodeau, Corpus Christianorum, Continuatio Mediaevalis 140A (Turnhout: Brepols, 1998), p. 9, ll. 6–22.

William Durand's reflections may appear otherworldly, but they are not far removed from the way an eminent contemporary liturgical scholar thinks about the matter. For, Joseph Ratzinger writes in his *Spirit of the Liturgy*:

> Worship gives us a share in heaven's mode of existence, in the world of God, and allows light to fall from that divine world into ours. In this sense, worship . . . has the character of anticipation.[51]

51 Joseph Ratzinger, *Theology of the Liturgy: The Sacramental Foundation of Christian Existence*, trans. John Saward et al., Collected Works 11 (San Francisco: Ignatius Press, 2014), 10 (*The Spirit of the Liturgy* forms Part A of this volume, pp. 1–150). In the German text, the word "heaven" appears in quotation marks: *Theologie der Liturgie. Die sakramentale Begründung christlicher Existenz*, Gesammelte Schriften 11 (Freiburg im Breisgau: Herder, 2008), 38. For an excellent introduction to Ratzinger's theology of the liturgy by one of his former students, one may read D. Vincent Twomey, SVD, *The Dynamics of Liturgy. Joseph Ratzinger's Theology of Liturgy: An Introduction* (San Francisco: Ignatius Press, 2022).

And a crucial anticipation: in anticipating the *telos* of human existence, worship "gives our present life its proper measure."[52] It tells us, to return to the phrase from William Durand, what to "imitate."

The question then becomes how such an imitation can be brought about. The answer points to the gulf that separates the liturgical subject from the Kantian one: the latter attempts to generate structures autonomously, spun out of its own rationality, whereas the former *receives* the Logos of its existence. Its life is "logicized" by an Other.[53] This Other is the Word Incarnate. In the celebration of the Eucharist, the Word who "clothed himself in a body"[54] to live among men takes on

52 *Theology of the Liturgy*, 10 / *Theologie der Liturgie*, 38. The German text lacks the word "proper."

53 The term "logicizing" is Ratzinger's; see *Theology of the Liturgy*, 34 / *Theologie der Liturgie*, 65.

54 This phrase is from a homily attributed to St. Macarius which appears in the Liturgy of the Hours; see *The Divine Office: The Liturgy of the Hours according to the Roman Rite*, vol. III: *Weeks of the Year 6–34* (London: Collins, 1974), Office of Readings, Week 34, Wednesday (p. 813). The

the appearance of bread and wine so that we may become incorporated into his Body. Bread and wine are masks, one could perhaps say, that the Lord takes on as a final step in his kenosis: eager to offer us salvation, to pull us into community with the Trinity, the Lord humbles himself to such a point that he appears as a mere thing, lowly food.[55] This

Greek phrase is ἐνδυσάμενος τὸ σῶμα (PG 34:712). The American translation is flat (as is so often the case in the American edition of the Divine Office): "He assumed a body" (*The Divine Office*, vol. IV: *Ordinary Time, Weeks 18–34* [New York: Catholic Book Publishing Corp., 1975], 596). Similarly, the Liturgy of the Hours features a sermon by St. Fulgentius of Ruspe for St. Stephen's Day where Fulgentius uses the same metaphor: "Yesterday our king put on the robe of flesh" (*The Divine Office: The Liturgy of the Hours according to the Roman Rite*, vol. I: *Advent, Christmastide, and Weeks 1–9 of the Year* [London: Collins, 1974]), 26 December, Office of Readings, Second Reading, p. 48*. The Latin phrase is *trabea carnis indutus* (PL 65:729C).

55 This is Jean-Luc Marion's interpretation of the "real" presence: the Lord becomes *res*, a "thing." See Marion, "La splendeur de la contemplation eucharistique," *Resurrection* 31

miracle is possible only because, in the words of consecration, the priest takes on the role of Christ himself, speaking the words of the Last Supper *in persona Christi*. "This is my body" and "This is my blood" are acts of performative speech. They do not *describe* the bread and wine offered on the altar but rather *make* them into "substances"—as the tradition says—quite different from what they appear to be. These words are action, as Ratzinger rightly points out: "This *oratio*—the Eucharistic Prayer, the 'Canon'—is really more than speech; it is *actio* in the highest sense of the word."[56] Who could have the authority to utter phrases that change reality at its deepest level, pulling things from "their creaturely anchorage"?[57] Only the Word through whom the world was created in the first place. The priest could certainly not

(1969): 84–8, and my article, "Postmodern Philosophy and J.-L. Marion's Eucharistic Realism," in *Transcendence and Phenomenology*, ed. Peter M. Candler, Jr., and Conor Cunningham, Veritas (London: SCM Press, 2007), 84–110.

56 Ratzinger, *Theology of the Liturgy*, 107/148.

57 Ibid.

bring about such a transformation on his own, merely human authority. "This is my body," uttered by the priest as human being, could not be a "happy" speech act.[58] In Ratzinger's words again, "He knows that he is now speaking, not from his own resources but, in virtue of the sacrament that he has received, he has become the voice of Someone Else, who is now speaking and acting."[59]

Putting on Christ

In his *Spirit of the Liturgy*, Ratzinger develops a brief but rich theology of clothes. He points

58 I am not aware of many attempts to place speech act theory in a Catholic context, except for some work by A. P. Martinich: "Sacraments and Speech Acts," *Heythrop Journal* 16 (1975): 289–303 (Part I) and 405–17 (Part II).

59 Ratzinger, *Theology of the Liturgy*, 107/148 (for better comprehension, I have moved a comma). The German text does not have "the voice of Someone Else," but simply *Stimme des anderen*, "voice of another." The difference is one of style: discreet in the case of the original, in-your-face in the translation.

to the frequent biblical references to the "putting on" of Christ or of the "new man."[60] This sartorial metaphor, he says, may well have been formed in analogy with the wearing of cultic masks in the religions of antiquity.[61] In the context of the liturgical celebration, the vestments that the priest

60 Gal. 3:27 (Χριστὸν ἐνεδύσασθε), Rom. 13:14 (ἐνδύσασθε τὸν Κύριον Ἰησοῦν Χριστόν), Eph. 4:24 (ἐνδύσασθαι τὸν καινὸν ἄνθρωπον), Col. 3:10 (καὶ ἐνδυσάμενοι τὸν νέον, τὸν ἀνακαινούμενον εἰς ἐπίγνωσιν κατ' εἰκόνα τοῦ κτίσαντος αὐτόν), 1 Cor. 15:53 (δεῖ γὰρ τὸ φθαρτὸν τοῦτο, ἐνδύσασθαι ἀφθαρσίαν; καὶ τὸ θνητὸν τοῦτο, ἐνδύσασθαι ἀθανασίαν). This language has significant background in the Psalms, where the image of clothes is even extended to the Lord himself, as in Psalm 103:1–2: "Bless the Lord, O my soul: O Lord my God, thou art exceedingly great, Thou hast put on praise and beauty and art clothed with light as with a garment."

61 Ratzinger, *Theology of the Liturgy*, 137–8/183: "The assumption is that the image of putting on Christ was developed by analogy with a man's putting on of the cultic mask of the deity when he was initiated into mystery cults." Unfortunately, Ratzinger does not provide a reference.

puts on symbolize that he stands in front of the congregation not as a private and sinful individual, but as someone who has clothed himself in Christ—wears the mask of Christ, we could say. But this is not a mask that conceals; it anticipates, just like the liturgy itself, the world to come. Does this make it unreal, a make-believe? Not at all. The priest, like all of us, is on the way to being more Christ-like, of becoming the mask that he is already wearing:[62]

> The image of putting on Christ is, therefore, a dynamic image, pointing to the transformation of man and the world, to the new humanity. Of all this—of this process of becoming Christ [*dieses Christuswerden*], and of the new community that is supposed to arise from it—the liturgical vestments

62 It is as Chad Engelland writes in "Unmasking the Person" (n. 1 above): "We deliberately act like something we inwardly are not yet and thereby become the very thing we were pretending to be" (457).

> are a reminder. They are a challenge to the priest to enter into the dynamism of an un-becoming [*Ent-Werdung*], out of the encapsulated self, and of becoming new [*Neuwerdung*] from Christ and toward Christ. They remind those who participate in the Mass of the new way that began with Baptism and continues with the Eucharist, toward the future world which, from the sacraments, is supposed to appear already in outline in our daily lives.[63]

Ratzinger's last sentence indicates that everything he says in this passage about the meaning of the priestly vestments applies to the layperson as well. For the layman or -woman, too, is engaged in a dynamic process of shedding the old self, with its inward bent, and embracing a new, more Christ-like self. Although in this life, this *Christuswerden* can

63 Ratzinger, *Theology of the Liturgy*, 138/183. I have amended the translation of this passage significantly.

never be complete, the sacraments—and the Eucharist, in particular—help us in rendering our everyday lives transparent toward the heavenly Jerusalem in which we hope to dwell one day.

The Temporality of the Liturgical Subject

The liturgical subject, then, lives in a space opened up by the tension between the present and the future, in the "between" that is the Church.[64] As St. Paul frames it in the First Letter to the Corinthians (7:29–31), he or she lives in a condition of "as if," endeavoring to render visible already in this world the splendor of the world to come:

> 29 This, therefore, I say, brethren;
> the time is short; it remaineth, that
> they also who have wives, be as if

64 Ibid., 32/62 and 56/90. The latter passage is rendered only approximatively in the English version.

> they had none; 30 And they that weep, as though they wept not; and they that rejoice, as if they rejoiced not; and they that buy, as though they possessed not; 31 And they that use this world, as if they used it not; for the fashion of this world passeth away.[65]

Shakespeare was right: all the world really is a stage, and the Christian subject is merely a player on it. Ratzinger himself is open to this idea. As he writes in the preface to *Spirit of the Liturgy*, one of his first readings after he embarked on his theological studies was Romano Guardini's influential little book entitled, like his own, *The Spirit of the Liturgy*—a book that "inaugurated the Liturgical

65 I comment in more detail on Paul's "as if not" (ὡς μὴ) in "A Brief Theology of the As If (Inspired by a Remark of Joseph Ratzinger)," in *Philosophos – Philotheos – Philoponos: Studies and Essays as Charisteria in Honor of Professor Bogoljub Šijaković on the Occasion of His 65th Birthday*, ed. Mikonja Knežević, in collaboration with Rade Kisić and Dušan Krcunović (Belgrade: Gnomon; Podgorica: Matica Srpska, 2021), 706–14.

Movement in Germany."[66] In one of the chapters of this influential book, Guardini suggested an understanding of the liturgy as play. Thus, it is no coincidence Ratzinger's own *Spirit of the Liturgy* opens with just that thought: that the liturgy is a form of play. He moves on after a couple of pages, noting that the play analogy is in the end too thin, lacking content, in particular concrete biblical content.[67] Still, he likes the analogy, writing about it in lyrical terms: "liturgy would be the

66 Ratzinger, *Theology of the Liturgy*, 3/30.

67 The English translation of *Spirit of the Liturgy* can be used only with great caution. In our current context, the translation reads: "But this analogy lacks something, something essential" (6). The German text however has, "Aber noch fehlt uns eine inhaltliche Füllung dieses Entwurfs" (33), which could be rendered as, "We still need to fill this sketch with content." In the English translation, Ratzinger appears to be distancing himself from Guardini's theory because of "essential" shortcomings, but in the German original, there is no mention of anything that is *wesentlich*. Rather, Ratzinger is saying that the theory does not have enough concrete content—which he then proceeds to supply. The difference is not merely one of nuance.

reawakening within us of true childhood, of openness to a greatness still to come, which is still unfulfilled in adult life . . . the life of freedom, of intimate union with God, of pure openness to our fellow-man. Thus it would imprint on the seemingly real life of daily existence the sign of true freedom, break open the walls that confine us, and let the light of heaven shine down upon earth."[68]

We need to return to our discussion of the temporal structure of the liturgical self. It lives in anticipation, such that its present is a "mixture of 'already' and 'not yet.'"[69] But how does it relate to the past? Here again the Eucharist is paradigmatic. In the celebration of the Eucharist, the foundational events of Christian worship—Christ's Cross and Resurrection—are no longer merely past: they are transferred into the present. This rendering present (*Vergegenwärtigung*)[70] means that

68 Ibid., 6/33; trans. amended. The translation renders Ratzinger's *Wiedererweckung* as "rediscovery," but that would be *Wiederentdeckung*.

69 Ibid., 32/63. I have moved the quotation marks to correspond to the German text.

70 Ibid., 34/65.

what occurred only once historically becomes contemporaneous with us as we celebrate the Eucharist: *semel* becomes *semper*, in Bernard of Clairvaux's words.[71] This transition from the "once" to the "always" is possible because to the external Passion of our Lord—his suffering and death on the Cross—there corresponds an inner, spiritual, and timeless act through which the Lord draws all of humanity into his love. In this manner, that which is a unique event in history transcends time, so that it can be repeated in, and brought back into, time: "The real interior act, which would not exist without the exterior, transcends time, but since it comes from time, time can again and again be brought into it. This is why contemporaneity is possible."[72]

Christ's Passion itself did not occur in a historical vacuum. It was—as Ratzinger impressively argues—the final step in the "inner dynamism of vetero-testamentarian history."[73] In the desire to reconnect with the

71 Ibid., 33/64.
72 Ibid.; trans. amended.
73 Ibid., 24/54; trans. amended.

Lord after the Fall, God's people moved from sacrifices of bulls to the understanding that what the Lord really wants is a pure heart. Since the Jews painfully felt the inadequacy of all material sacrifices, the Old Testament's sacrificial system was "constantly accompanied by prophetic disquiet and questioning."[74] When Jesus becomes the Paschal Lamb, he therefore assumes and sublates the cultic crisis of ancient Israel, indeed "of the whole ancient world."[75] He is the last and eternal sacrifice, in which all vain attempts to placate God by means of human offerings are replaced by the Lord's offer to take us with him back to the Father: "And I, if I be lifted up from the earth, will draw all things to myself" (John 12:32). In this way, the true essence of sacrifice becomes clear: "returning to love and therefore divinization."[76]

74 Ibid., 22/52.

75 Ibid., 27/57.

76 Ibid., 19/48: "Einkehr in die Liebe . . . und so Vergöttlichung." The word *Einkehr*, literally "turning inside," has connotations both of a turning inward and of a coming home to a place of hospitality.

The human being who puts on Christ, and is assumed into his Body in the Eucharist, participates in this dynamism—not only insofar as it points forward, but also insofar as it comes from the depths of Old Testament history. The liturgical subject, then, is historical through and through; its encounter with the Lord and its journey home do not occur in the atemporal space of an encapsulated self. It has to be this way. For, Ratzinger declares, the essence of the human being is inextricably historical:

> For indeed, man is historically shaped, from the ground up; it is precisely his *essence* to be *historical*: one cannot contrast a timelessly enduring essence with the change and chance of history without misunderstanding man fundamentally, for in him history and essence coincide and the one is real only in the other.[77]

77 Ratzinger, "The Sacramental Foundation of Christian Existence," in *Theology of the Liturgy*, 153–68, at 163; corresponding to "Die sakra-

It is striking to read this paragraph from the pen of a thinker who is often placed in the "conservative" camp of modern theology. But then, why does he write like a historicist, rather than maintaining the reality of an eternal, unchangeable human essence? The reason is that Ratzinger was, from his doctoral research through his entire career, a theologian of history. For him, Christianity is all dynamism: the "history of God with men," as he likes to say.[78] This is a fascinating topic, but unfortunately not one that we can pursue in the present context.[79]

mentale Begründung christlicher Existenz," in *Theologie der Liturgie*, 197–214, at 208. Translation lightly amended; emphasis original.

78 The formula recurs frequently. See, for example, *Introduction to Christianity*, trans. J. R. Foster (London: Search Press, 1969), 257: "teaching about the Church must take its departure from teaching about the Holy Spirit and his gifts. But its goal lies in a doctrine of the history of God with men or, alternatively, of the function of the story of Christ for mankind as a whole."

79 I have written about the roots of Ratzinger's theology in "The Young Ratzinger," in *Oxford Handbook on Joseph Ratzinger*, ed. Francesca

What we should do, however, is briefly consider the continuation of the extract just quoted:

> Let us say it more concretely: my humanity is realized in the word, in the language that shapes my thought and initiates me into the social community that shapes my own humanity. Language, however, which we may thus describe as an essential medium for the realization of human existence, it not something I myself create; indeed, it fulfills its purpose precisely through and in the fact that it unites me with the people around me and with the people before me: language is the expression of the continuity of the human spirit in the historical unfolding of its essence.[80]

Murphy and Tracey Rowland (New York: Oxford University Press, forthcoming).

80 Ratzinger, *Theology of the Liturgy*, 163/208. I have amended the English translation, which is

We have here, in Ratzinger's theology of the liturgy, an attempt to think "at the same time, without discontinuity or contradiction, the being of man and the being of language."[81] This is possible only because, for the Christian, language is ultimately rooted in the Logos, the Word. It is not only through the Word that all being was created, but the Word also became man. The Word/word, man, and being are thus intimately connected.

misleading in many ways. For instance, it renders the last word, "essence" (*Wesen* in German), as "nature." But that would be *Natur*.

81 The quotation is from Foucault; see n. 27 above.

III

The Constitution of Catholic Time and Space

The fundamental temporal structure of the liturgical subject is now clear. Taking up man's historically constituted essence, the liturgy clothes it in Christ, to make it ever more Christ-like and bring it home. This is a technology of the self, but one in which the ultimate initiative is God's, not man's. Responding to God's offer of salvation, the human being lets him- or herself be shaped into a particular form of temporal existence, one whose *telos* lies, paradoxically, outside of time.

The purpose of this third section is to fill the idea of this liturgical form of temporal existence with more concrete content. The goal is to bring out in more detail the specifics of what I call, in shorthand, "Catholic time." For if it is true, as we said at the beginning of the previous section, that the liturgy is simply all of life, considered teleologically, then the temporal structure of the liturgical subject must in some way permeate everyday existence. This is what I attempt to show. In a second step, I turn to Catholic space, since time and space together form the basic parameters in which embodied life occurs.

Making such an argument about the distinctiveness of Catholic time and space requires at least a brief treatment of other forms of living temporally and spatially. So we now turn to an overview of modes of temporal existence, in order to contrast them with Catholic time. This requires a more descriptive, phenomenological type of approach, at least initially.

Catholic Time among the Modes of Temporal Existence

Natural Time. For human beings, as for other animals, the most natural rhythm of time is the circadian cycle of day and night. The human body is constituted in such a way that it is most vigorous and alert during daytime, when there is light, while it switches to a resting mode in its absence. This is why the most basic unit of time is the day.

The rising and setting of the sun which demarcate day from night embed human life in the cosmic order, in that one cycle of day and night corresponds to one complete rotation of the earth. In other words, our biological clock is regulated by cosmic forces. Similarly, a month is the time it takes the moon to orbit the earth, and a year is the time it takes the earth to complete its orbit of the sun. Since the earth's rotation has an axial tilt in relation to its orbital plane, some parts of the earth are more titled toward the sun than others, depending on where the earth is in its orbit. This combination of the earth's own tilted rotation and its orbit around the sun is responsible for the biologically crucial rhythm of the seasons.

There are other units of biological time, but these are more specific to the functioning of particular organisms. So, for example, the lifespan of a human is longer than that of a mosquito but shorter than that of an oak tree; the periods of gestation of different species of mammals are of varying length; the rhythm of the beating heart or the breathing lungs varies across species as well. Different forms of life, therefore, live in accordance with different rhythms, yet none escapes the cosmic order.

Technological Time. Only humans have attempted to detach themselves from this cosmic order by creating technologies of time. Put differently, all animals have a circadian rhythm, but only human beings are capable of measuring and mastering their rhythm of day and night.

This measuring and mastering began with the construction of the first sundials. Not every sundial necessarily measures the units of a day; indeed, the earliest sundials were devoted to larger rhythms. They were constructed to allow human beings to observe the "movements" of the sun as it regulated the seasons. The verb "observe" carries two meanings in this context: "to notice" or "to perceive," but also the meaning that we have in mind when we speak of someone "observing" a holy day. It was not idle curiosity, for example, which had an Irish tribe build the neolithic monument of Newgrange in County Meath, a monument constructed in such a way that the central chamber is illuminated by the sun almost exactly on the day of the winter solstice (and a couple of days before and after). We no longer know the exact purpose of this arrangement, but the presence of graves in the complex suggests a connection with a religious rite.[82] Thousands of years later, the technological innovations that led to the creation of cutting-edge clocks and astrolabes in the Muslim world were driven by the desire to pray at exactly the right times of the day, and to do so facing in the correct direction.[83] The

82 For reflections on the religious experience induced by the play of sunlight in the central chamber, see Robert Hensey, *First Light: The Origins of Newgrange*, Oxbow Insights in Archaeology (Oxford: Oxbow Books, 2015), esp. chap. 4: "Waiting for the Sun" (66–78).

83 The title of the standard work on this subject is

situation in medieval Europe was no different: it is in monasteries that the first mechanical clocks were used to help determine the correct hours for the performance of the liturgy. Let us not forget this point: our technologies of time measurement have grown from religious roots.

In the history of technological time, we have come a long way since the sundial. By way of sand clocks and water clocks, pendulum clocks, balance-wheel clocks, and quartz clocks we have reached the age of the atomic clock, where seconds are measured in terms of the frequency of the radiation emitted by particular atoms. Thus, time is still measured through natural rhythms, but these rhythms have become much faster and can be observed only by high-powered instruments. Once upon a time, the length of a day was determined by the rising and setting of the

telling: David A. King, *In Synchrony with the Heavens: Studies in Astronomical Timekeeping and Instrumentation in Medieval Islamic Civilization*, 2 vols., Islamic Philosophy, Theology and Science. Texts and Studies 55 (Leiden: Brill, 2004/2005).

sun; now a second is defined as the unperturbed ground-state hyperfine transition frequency of the cesium 133 atom, that is, 9,192,631,700 Hz.[84]

This definition, in its extreme abstraction, draws our attention to a phenomenon that has been well-known by philosophers since the nineteenth century: the more technologically advanced and industrialized human life becomes—the more we are able to master our "environment"—the more likely are we to experience alienation. Just as the factory worker laboring at the conveyor belt risks being alienated from the products of his labor (as Marx famously argued), so we risk being alienated from time. It is not

84 For a brief and accessible history of time-keeping, see James Jespersen and Jane Fitz-Randolph, *From Sundials to Atomic Clocks: Understanding Time and Frequency*, 2nd rev. ed. (Garden City: Dover, 1999). The standard work on the interaction between technologies of time and the modern experience of time is Gerhard Dohrn-van Rossum, *History of the Hour: Clocks and Modern Temporal Orders*, trans. Thomas Dunlap (Chicago: University of Chicago Press, 1996).

only that we no longer understand how it is measured and where it comes from. We frequently live alienated from our own biological clocks: we work night shifts made possible by artificial light and therefore don't sleep when our circadian rhythm suggests we should; we are jet-lagged after long-distance travel; we experience the biological clock of aging as a threat and attempt to slow it down, stop it, or turn it back rather than embracing the finite duration of our existence. We even try to master the times of birth and of death, in the process assimilating the human body to a machine that can be turned on and off at will. In this way, the attempt to master time turns against us, as we end up being mastered by the very technologies that we devised to throw off our finitude.

Cultural Time. A final modality of time that we should consider before moving on to Catholic time is what one could call "cultural" time. This is the time of memory, especially collective memory. While cultural time is not independent of natural and technological time, its distinctiveness stems from the fact that it must distinguish significant events from those insignificant ones that are not worth being remembered. Cultural time finds its clearest expression in the writing of history, but long before history was invented as a discipline, bards sang of the deeds of warriors and kings, prophets told stories about divine interventions on earth, generals wrote about their exploits on the battlefield, and monks chronicled the happenings in and around their monasteries.[85] In these literary genres, time is culturally appropriated to situate the self in a larger community.

Just like natural time, cultural time has entered a crisis because the construction of the total memory that is the internet makes it ever more difficult to distinguish what matters from what does not, at both the individual and at the collective levels. In the

85 In the introduction to his lectures on the philosophy of history, Hegel offers a well-known taxonomy of history-writing, distinguishing "original," "reflective," and "philosophical" approaches to history, with several subdivisions.

past, technologies to exteriorize memory were limited and slow: to make sure I remembered a significant event, I could record it in a journal or paste a photo into an album. If I was so gifted, I could compose a poem or create a painting. Now, however, all my memories, in the form of thousands of photographs as well as endless streams of tweets and posts, reside in the so-called "cloud." Overwhelmed by the amount of data, I lose myself in them, dispersed in a flood of information that I myself have created. No wonder philosophers of the digital age are beginning to consider the importance of forgetting.[86]

Catholic Time. At the very beginning of the revealed Word, the opening lines of the Book of Genesis present God as the creator of day and night:

> [1] In the beginning God created
> heaven, and earth. [2] And the earth

86 On this topic, see Viktor Mayer-Schönberger, *Delete: The Virtue of Forgetting in the Digital Age* (Princeton: Princeton University Press, 2009).

> was void and empty, and darkness was upon the face of the deep; and the spirit of God moved over the waters. [3] And God said: Be light made. And light was made. [4] And God saw the light that it was good; and he divided the light from the darkness. [5] And he called the light Day, and the darkness Night; and there was evening and morning one day. (Gen. 1:1–5)

When Christians observe a day of rest, they do so to live in accordance with the rhythm of the created order, in which the seventh day was a day of repose: "And on the seventh day God ended his work which he had made: and he rested on the seventh day from all the work which he had done" (Gen. 2:2). One could object that the Genesis narrative is just a story, a myth, and that God could not have created the world in six days, followed by a sabbath, because God does not exist in time. This is certainly correct. The Genesis narrative does not offer a scientific account, but is concerned with the orientation of the created order toward the Creator. The Fourth Commandment asks us to "keep holy the sabbath day" (Exod. 20:8), so that to the gift of creation there corresponds a response of homage and praise offered to the Creator. In more contemporary philosophical terms, the sabbath could be described as an acknowledgment of human finitude and heteronomy. This was already its meaning in ancient Judaism; in the New Covenant, the day of rest—now the Sunday—is also the day of the Resurrection, which means, to cite Joseph Ratzinger again, that it becomes "the sign of God's definitive world, in which shadow and image are superseded in the final mutual indwelling of God and his creatures."[87] We can see here how cosmic time, which from the very beginning is God's time, is progressively saturated with religious significance and sanctified.

The whole point of the Christian structuring of time—of which the observance of Sunday is perhaps the most obvious example—is

87 Ratzinger, *Theology of the Liturgy*, 60/94

to allow the believer to conform the rhythm of his or her life to God's time: "Sunday is thus, for the Christian, time's proper measure, the temporal measure of his life."[88] But what is God's time? It is indeed the time of day and night, the rhythm of the created order, but it is also more: it is, as we already discussed earlier, the time of God's history with his people. This story is narrated—sometimes mythologically, sometimes historically, always devoutly—in the Scriptures. The two parts into which the Christian Scriptures are divided, the Old Testament and the New, correspond to two phases in God's history with his people. In the Old Testament, we learn of the Lord's relationship with the people of Israel; in the New, that relationship is—on the Christian understanding, to be sure—deepened or, to use a scriptural term, "fulfilled" (Matt. 5:17). The fulfillment consists in the fact that the restoration of the kingdom of Israel, with Jerusalem and Mount Zion at its center, has occurred in the person of Jesus Christ, although with the crucial

88 Ibid.

difference that we are no longer dealing with a political structure and geographical boundaries. "My kingdom is not of this world" (John 18:36), Jesus says. Not only is this kingdom not of his world; it is also present in a merely incipient form, awaiting completion at the end of time.

The scriptural perspective that we have now adopted confirms what we said earlier about the temporal structure of the liturgical subject: Christians live time in a manner that is both forward-looking and backward-looking. In the Old Testament, we find indications of the providential presence of the Lord in the history of the people of Israel. In the same Old Testament, however, we also discover intimations of the fulfillment of that history in the life of God become man. Thus, the Christian experience of time is backward-looking precisely as it is forward-looking, discovering the future in the past. The present is constituted at the intersection of these two perspectives. This is why a central element of the liturgy is the juxtaposition of passages from the Old and New Testaments. The present arises from their dialogue. "But there is no real future here," one could object: both Testaments are closed. The events narrated in the New Testament occurred two thousand years ago while the Old Testament reaches back into the mythical realm of the foundation of the world. How can one get a future out of their interaction? Here, a point already hinted at becomes crucial: the kingdom is still awaiting completion in the interval between the Ascension and the Second Coming. The history of God with his people is ongoing. According to a well-established theological phrase, the kingdom exists "already not yet."[89] Or, as Ratzinger says, the Church militant exists in a state "in-between." The time which is not yet complete needs structure, which is generated by the interpretation of the two Testaments in light of each other.[90]

89 The term goes back to Oscar Cullmann's classical study, *Christ and Time: The Primitive Christian Conception of Time and History*, trans. Floyd V. Filson (Philadelphia: Westminster Press, 1950).

90 This structure was the subject matter of Ratzinger's *Habilitationsschrift*, his "second doctoral dissertation," which was devoted to

If the notion of the "already not yet" is paradoxical, there is an even larger paradox: the entire aim of a Christian life in accordance with the rhythm of God's time is to move beyond time. For the kingdom which is not of this world is a timeless one where God's people praise the Lord in eternal simultaneity: "But of this one thing be not ignorant, my beloved," says the Second Letter of St. Peter, "that one day with the Lord is as a thousand years, and a thousand years as one day" (2 Pet. 3:8). This timeless end of Christian time distinguishes it from both natural time, which is cyclical, and technological time, which proceeds toward an ever-receding horizon of progress.

Yet Christian time also remains cyclical, going as it does beyond natural time without attempting to erase it. One could speak of a Christian fulfillment, "sublation,"[91] or sanctification

Bonaventure's theology of history. I discuss the *Habilitationsschrift* in "The Young Ratzinger" (see n. 78 above).

91 "Sublation" translates the Hegelian term *Aufhebung*, which in turn hearkens back to the biblical

of natural time. A Christian day remains a day, and a Christian year, a year. But the liturgy projects onto the cycle of natural time a cycle in which the most significant events of salvation history are remembered, repeated, and re-enacted.

The liturgical year begins on the First Sunday of Advent—that is to say, in the expectation of the birth of the Savior—and culminates in the Easter season, which celebrates his Resurrection, Ascension into heaven, and gift of the Spirit. The date of Christmas connects its celebration with the winter solstice in the northern hemisphere, for Jesus is "light from light," according to the Nicene Creed. So nothing could be more appropriate than to celebrate his birth at a time when, even naturally, more light comes into the world. Easter, on the other hand, ties the Christian religious calendar back to its Jewish roots since the events of Easter

notion of fulfillment. A sublation cancels what it sublates even as it maintains it and elevates it to a higher level—in accordance with the three semantic dimensions of the German verb *aufheben*.

unfolded when Jesus entered Jerusalem with his disciples to celebrate Passover. Passover, in turn, is a moveable feast, and just like Easter is determined by the lunar cycle. Again, religious time does not supersede cosmic time, but builds upon it. *Gratia non tollit naturam,* as Thomas Aquinas formulates in the *Summa*: "grace does not cancel nature"—and he adds: *sed perficit,* "but perfects it."[92] The Thomistic principle identifies a crucial difference between sacred time—that is, God's time—and merely human technologies of time. As we have seen, the latter carry the risk of occluding natural cycles, in the process throwing human beings "out of sync," as it were, with their inherent, biological temporality, which in turn mirrors the temporality of the cosmos. What ensues is alienation of the human being from itself, the cosmos, and God.

92 The phrase occurs very early on in the *Summa,* as a fundamental methodological principle: "Cum enim gratia non tollat naturam, sed perficit, oportet quod naturalis ratio subserviat fidei" (*ST* I, qu. 1, art. 8, ad 2).

The liturgical year, by contrast, is a technology of the self that does not disrupt the cosmic order but, through the sanctification of natural rhythms of time, draws the believer into salvation history and, ultimately, into the life of God himself.[93] The practicing Catholic rejoices with the Holy Family on Christmas Day, suffers with Christ on Good Friday (and every Friday), and on Easter Sunday (and every Sunday) experiences the joy of the Resurrection. Every week or even day, at the celebration of the Eucharist, he or she is assumed into the Body of Christ, and lives again how the Lord gave his body and poured out his blood to heal the wounds of sin.

In the Catholic tradition, the most audacious attempt to subsume natural time into God's time, and thus to deify the

93 Both the Orthodox and the Catholic traditions go so far as to speak of deification as the goal of Christian life, and indeed of creation as a whole. As Ratzinger puts it, "the goal of worship and the goal of creation as a whole are one and the same—divinization, a world of freedom and love" (*Theology of the Liturgy*, 15/44).

temporal order, is the Liturgy of the Hours. Since the first Christian centuries until the present, albeit with modifications, the Liturgy of the Hours has structured the day of those called to the religious or ordained life. From Matins, which were (and in some religious orders, still are), said in the early morning hours before sunrise, to Compline at the end of the day, the canonical hours call the believer to prayer and praise at regular intervals. The juxtaposition of readings from the Psalms, which make up the bulk of each Hour, with texts from the New Testament and the tradition of the Church distributes the characteristic Christian schema of time into almost every living hour. In this fashion, time lived here on earth becomes a foretaste of the timelessness of the kingdom.

The technology of the self that is enacted in the Liturgy of the Hours is structurally analogous to the celebration of the Eucharist. Just as in the latter, the celebrant "puts on" Christ and at the culmination of the ceremony speaks *in persona Christi*, so the believer who recites the Liturgy of the

Hours takes on the role of the psalmist. The liturgical subject suffers with the psalmist when he feels abandoned by God, gives thanks with him when the Lord's grace returns, praises the Lord with him for his great glory, or asks God with him for mercy and assistance. In this way, the liturgist is inserted into the history of ancient Israel, the nation whom the Lord chose and guided as his flock. Finally, in assuming the psalmist's voice, the liturgist also joins Christ's voice, for Christ himself prayed the Psalms, both in the synagogue and at crucial points in his life.[94] To describe this role play, the late Angelus Häußling, leading authority on the Liturgy of the Hours, employed the term "role identification": "Praying the Psalms is not the utterance of

94 This paragraph is informed by the excellent work of Angelus A. Häußling, OSB, *Tagzeitenliturgie in Geschichte und Gegenwart. Historische und theologische Studien*, ed. Martin Klöckener, 2nd ed., Liturgiewissenschaftliche Quellen und Forschungen 100 (Münster: Aschendorff, 2017), esp. the chapter "Die Übung der Tagzeiten in der Geschichte der Kirche" (52–68).

some sort of pious sentences before God, but a role identification of the Christian with his Christ."[95]

Häußling laments the decline of the Liturgy of the Hours in the life of the contemporary Church. Since the 1960s, "even the priests' praying of the breviary has become rare"[96] (who has in recent years spotted a priest perambulating with the open breviary?), not to mention the total absence of the Liturgy of the Hours in parish life. And something else is surprising, namely, the complete silence on the topic of the Liturgy of the Hours in an influential and much-admired work that we already know well: *The Spirit of the Liturgy* by Joseph Ratzinger. The reader of this book could easily walk away with the impression that there was no Liturgy of the Hours in the Catholic

95 Angelus A. Häußling, OSB, *Christliche Identität aus der Liturgie. Theologische und historische Studien zum Gottesdienst der Kirche*, ed. Martin Klöckner et al., Liturgiewissenschaftliche Quellen und Studien 79 (Münster: Aschendorff, 1997), 7.

96 Häußling, *Tagzeitenliturgie*, 65.

Church.[97] But without it, how are parishes, and the Christians in them, going to be initiated into a daily order of prayer? That is Häußling's urgent question.[98]

A Note on Liturgical Language. To round out this overview of the Catholic experience of time, we need to return to the topic of language. For the schema here sketched out to work, language must function figuratively. We have established how Christian time fulfills both natural time and the time of the Old Testament. "Fulfillment" means that the order of nature and the Old Covenant prefigure Christian realities. To use the language of the tradition, the Book of Nature and the Book of Scripture need to be read together,

97 This is one of the criticisms Häußling advances of *The Spirit of the Liturgy* in his detailed review: "Der Geist der Liturgie. Zu Joseph Ratzingers gleichnamiger Publikation," *Archiv für Liturgiewissenschaft* 43/44 (2001/2002): 362–95. Another is Ratzinger's failure to engage with the Vatican Council's Constitution on the Sacred Liturgy, *Sacrosanctum concilium*.

98 See Häußling, *Tagzeitenliturgie*, 65.

since they illuminate each other. So, for example, the Liturgy of the Hours features readings from Exodus during the Lenten period because the Lord's gracious actions in enabling Israel's flight from Egypt and liberation from Pharaoh's rule are a figure of the liberation from sin that occurs through Jesus' sacrifice on the Cross. Liturgical texts often describe the Cross as the "tree of life," as by Jesus's death and resurrection the wood of death is miraculously transformed into a living tree full of sap. Thus, by grace the Lord gives access to the same tree of life which in Genesis 3 was off limits—because Adam and Eve attempted sinful self-divinization.

We can see here a web of figurative meanings that keeps oscillating between the Old and New Covenants, on the one hand, and the natural world, on the other. Salvation history and the cosmic order form a single text written by the Creator and pointing to him—indeed, moving back to him. The Psalms, in particular, are rich in images that tell a single story of cosmos, man, and God. The psalmist likens the Lord to a bird and is hoping to take refuge in the shadow of his wings (Ps. 56:2). The soul yearns for God like deer that yearn for running streams (Ps. 41:2). Everything comes alive, such that mountains leap like rams and hills like yearling sheep (Ps. 113:3). As Ratzinger puts it, in this vision of the cosmos, things become more than things; the world acquires a transparency toward salvation history and its Creator.[99]

For Ratzinger, the cosmic dimension of liturgical language is absolutely central. There cannot be a break between salvation history and the cosmic order, because the function of worship is "to draw the whole of reality into communion with God."[100] Indeed, for Ratzinger the specifically Christian

99 See Ratzinger, "The Sacramental Foundation of Human Existence," 161/207 ("Things are more than things") and 153/198 ("symbolic transparency of reality toward the eternal").

100 Ratzinger, *Theology of the Liturgy*, 14/43. The cosmic dimension of salvation is the focus of Wayne Hankey's *PANTOKRATOR, the Cosmic Christ: A Christian Theology of Nature* (Charlottetown, Prince Edward Island: St. Peter Publications, [2004]).

dimension of worship lies in the fact that the liturgy brings together cosmos and salvation history: "For the Christian sacraments mean not only insertion into the God-permeated cosmos . . . they mean at the same time insertion into the history that comes from Christ."[101]

A lot is at stake here. Does the liturgy remain a viable technology of the self once its language becomes unintelligible? Few nowadays are sufficiently well-versed in Old Testament history to understand the logic behind the liturgical combination of Old and New Testament passages. Furthermore, modern man speaks an impoverished language that is cut off from metaphor. Each thing coincides with itself. It just is what it is, not a sign of another. This development reflects the scientific understanding of language, in which each term is defined univocally as carrying exactly one meaning. But even popular culture tends toward univocity. Consider the way people in the Western world tend to

101 Ratzinger, "The Sacramental Foundation of Christian Existence," 162/208; trans. amended.

dress. It is no longer the case that "clothes make the man," as Gottfried Keller suggested in the title of his famous novella—that is to say, that the clothes we wear represent a particular place in the social order. Most of the time, what we wear is simply meant to be comfortable or "authentic." The consequence is that our clothes lose their significance; indeed, often enough they are reduced to so little that only bare corporeality remains. In such a culture, who can understand the notion of "putting on Christ," or the meaning that the vestments of a priest carry?

In conclusion, the fate of the Church in the modern world is to a significant extent a question of language.

Catholic Space among the Modes of Spatial Existence

Just like the Catholic experience of time, the Catholic manner of constituting space exists among several other modes of spatial existence. Sketching these modes will provide the necessary context for our discussion of Catholic space.

Natural Space. All animals not only take a place in the natural order but shape it. Worms and moles create tunnels below ground, spiders build webs in which to catch their prey, and beavers construct dams to improve their habitat. As Psalm 84 declares, "The sparrow herself finds a home and the swallow a nest for her brood."[102] Human houses, towns, and roads are not fundamentally different—or perhaps we should say, *were* not fundamentally different. Geologists have come to the conclusion that human intervention in the created order has reached a point such that it may make sense to speak of the "Anthropocene" as a distinct geological period. Human alteration of the natural order has led to phenomena such as the homogenization of ecosystems (as globalization spreads species around the globe), reduction of biodiversity,

102 Quoted from the *The Liturgy of the Hours*, vol. III (n. 51 above), Week 3, Monday, Morning Prayer (p. [285]).

and changes in the rhythm of day and night in non-human organisms due to light pollution. Climate change comes under this rubric as well, along with a plethora of other phenomena that are expected to create a distinct geological record.

Anthropocene or not, the fact of the matter is that the relentless spread of human settlement and infrastructure now largely precludes the discovery of any part of the created order on earth that has not been affected by human intervention. As Henri Lefebvre writes, "nature is now seen as merely the raw material out of which the productive forces of a variety of social systems have forged their particular spaces."[103] And so we turn to technological space.

103 Henri Lefebvre, *The Production of Space*, trans. Donald Nicholson-Smith (Malden, MA: Blackwell, 1991), 31. Lefebvre's *magnum opus* is of limited use for our purposes because of its rather rigidly Marxist approach. Moreover, while many of his analyses of neo-capitalist space are incisive, Lefebvre has very little to say about religious space.

Technological Space. As just noted, human beings have always created structures and infrastructures to make the earth their home. In doing so, they use tools, so that human building is technological in a way that animals' building activities are not. What distinguishes the Anthropocene from earlier periods in the human shaping of nature is that, since the rise of industrialization and accelerated urbanization in the nineteenth century, human structures and infrastructures have reduced natural space entirely to resource.[104] We have overlaid natural space with a web of conduits—roads and highways, pipelines, electric transmission lines, telephone and data cables, shipping lines,

104 Resource is what Lefebvre calls "material" in the passage just quoted. Heidegger calls it *Bestand* (translated, a bit clumsily, as "standing-reserve") in "The Question concerning Technology," trans. William Lovitt, in *Basic Writings*, ed. David Farrell Krell (New York: Harper Collins, 1993), 311–41. For the German text, see Heidegger, *Vorträge und Aufsätze (1936–1953)*, ed. Friedrich-Wilhelm von Herrmann, Gesamtausgabe 7 (Frankfurt am Main: Klostermann, 2000), 7–36 (esp. 17).

transmission towers and satellites connected by electric waves, air transportation routes—in which resources for production and consumption circulate around the globe. Everything thus moved risks losing its internal coherence and integrity:[105] just as fossilized and crystallized carbon rock is mined, shipped to power plants, and transformed into energy, so the data harvested from humans are collected in data centers, traded, and exploited for the optimization of sales of goods and services.[106] Even natural spaces that we try to preserve in a more or less pristine state, like state parks, are absorbed into the circulatory system as destinations for the tourism industry. It is just as Wolfgang

105 Heidegger speaks of *das Gegenstandslose,* "objectlessness," to describe the dissolution of objects in a web of resources (ibid., 324/19 and 332/ 27).

106 Shoshana Zuboff terms this exploitation of human data for commercial purposes "surveillance capitalism." See Zuboff, *The Age of Surveillance Capitalism: The Fight for a Human Future at the New Frontier of Power* (New York: Public Affairs, 2019).

Schivelbusch puts it in the final sentence of his remarkable study on the transformation of space and time brought about by railway travel, "For the twentieth-century tourist, the world has become one huge department store of countrysides and cities."[107]

The essential difference between rural and urban spaces boils down to the density of human structure and infrastructure. A village not only consists of fewer buildings than a city, but these buildings are networked with each other and with the surrounding world in a looser infrastructural web. Indeed, a remote village may boast its own well, and dwellings located outside its community may have individual septic tanks. A dwelling that is entirely off-grid even generates its own electricity and heat—or, in a more radical case, may try to do without electricity at all.

Why are people in our own, technologically advanced age often drawn to the country,

107 Wolfgang Schivelbusch, *The Railway Journey: The Industrialization of Time and Space in the Nineteenth Century.* With a New Preface (Oakland, CA: University of California Press, 2014), 197.

that is, away from the centers of consumption, production, and power where they live and work? The answer is that the reduction of every element of the created order to resource—not least the reduction of people to "human resources" or even "human capital"—is profoundly alienating. Just as our attempts to master time have turned against us in that we have become slaves to technological time, so our mastery of space has left us uprooted and homeless.[108] Instead of dwelling somewhere, we circulate in the system. We have "transferrable skills," not work that corresponds to a vocation. As we keep moving from place to place, too many of us do not live in homesteads, but are stored in housing "units."

108 The mastery of space and time are intimately connected in a way that we cannot further investigate in the present context. It is clear, for example, that the ability to traverse space in less and less time (by means of trains, cars, and airplanes) fundamentally changes the rhythm of human life. *The Railway Journey*, by the German cultural historian Wolfgang Schivelbusch (see previous note), is devoted to this topic.

This homelessness is even more pronounced in the most recent and advanced form of technological space that has come to dominate our lives: digital space. Digital space represents the attempt not merely to transform natural space, but to supplant it altogether. In digital space, we have conversations with people on the other side of the globe as though we were chatting with neighbors—but the participants in the exchange are disincarnate. They cannot touch or smell each other, and they will be at different points in their circadian cycles. To make matters worse, the "room" in which they meet is not only immaterial, but often enough counterfactual, that is to say, contradicting the physical world. So, for example, it has become fashionable not to receive partners in online conversations in the actual space in which the conversation is recorded—say, a living room or a study—but to choose an artificial background scene instead. Thus, a person in Kentucky conducting an online conversation with a friend in Ireland could choose a Bavarian mountain scene as background, in eager anticipation of an upcoming vacation in Germany. One could delve further into computer games that take place in an entirely imaginary space where players select avatars to represent them in virtual reality. It would be interesting to investigate how exactly this scenario differs from older forms of role play, like the ones that have been central in our earlier discussions.[109]

Architectural Space. But our discussion requires further nuance. There must be a way of living in space that is properly human without being destructive. This way goes beyond animals' ability to transform their habitat and yet does not reduce nature to resource. What is at stake is the possibility that human beings can make nature a

109 There is beginning to be significant scholarly discussion about the theological significance of the digital revolutions. One of the pioneers in this field is Antonio Spadaro SJ with his *Cybertheology: Thinking Christianity in the Era of the Internet,* trans. Maria Way (Bronx, NY: Fordham University Press, 2014).

genuine home, one shared with all of creation.[110] To put this in Ratzinger's terms,

> "Subdue the earth!" (Gen. 1:28). This does not mean: Enslave it! Exploit it! Do with it what you will! No, what it does mean is: Recognize it as God's gift! Guard it and look after it, as sons look after what they have inherited from their father. Look after it, so that it becomes truly God's garden [*Gottesgarten*] and its inner meaning is fulfilled.[111]

This text is beautiful, but it does not bring us closer to understanding how the human calling to transform the earth into a *Gottesgarten* can be put into practice. For that, we turn to Heidegger.

In one of his most famous essays—a

110 Hence the subtitle of Pope Francis's encyclical *Laudato Si': On Our Care for Our Common Home* (2015).

111 Ratzinger, *Theology of the Liturgy*, 59/93; trans. amended.

piece that has become the foundation of a Heideggerian current in contemporary architectural theory[112]—the philosopher talks about a bridge in a landscape. Our common conception of a bridge would be of a piece of architecture that makes it possible for humans to cross something that is "in the way," such as a river, valley, or road. Then, we might add the aspect of beauty to this utilitarian consideration: a bridge fulfills its function and then, on top of that, it can be beautiful or ugly. But this is not at all how Heidegger approaches the bridge. He claims that the bridge has a *revealing* function: "The bridge swings over the stream 'with ease and power.' It does not just connect banks that are already there," he writes. "The banks emerge as banks only as the bridge crosses the stream." What is more, the entire landscape lying behind the banks appears as

112 One of the best-known representatives of this current is Christian Norberg-Schulz, who taught at the University of Dallas in the 1980s. Among his many books, see for example *Genius Loci: Towards a Phenomenology of Architecture* (New York: Rizzoli, 1980).

such only because of the bridge. In summarizing, Heidegger declares that the bridge "gathers the earth as landscape around the stream."[113]

In Heidegger's way of thinking, the bridge is not a human artefact that is added to its surroundings in some extrinsic manner, perhaps aesthetically pleasing or not pleasing. Rather, the bridge lets the entire landscape appear. In fact, the bridge is that which gives rise to place: "Thus the bridge does not first come to a place to stand in it; rather, a place comes into existence only by virtue of the bridge."[114] And then, from the place, space is opened up. This is the real space in which humans can feel at home, or "dwell." By contrast, the scientific notion of space—

113 Heidegger, "Building Dwelling Thinking," in *Basic Writings*, 343–63 (at 354). The German text appears in *Vorträge und Aufsätze*, 145–64. The first sentence contains a quotation from a poem by Hölderlin, "Lange lieb' ich dich schon," an ode to his beloved Heidelberg.

114 Ibid., 356/156. The English text has "locale" for Heidegger's *Ort*, but "place" is a much more natural translation.

extension in three dimensions—is a mere abstraction.

As I said, for Heidegger the essential function of building is to *reveal*. And that is what sets humans apart from animals: in Chad Engelland's words, "we are entrusted with the structure of revealing-concealing."[115] Thus, authentic dwelling entails the creation of places and the opening up of space—it involves letting things *be*—whereas the technological reduction of natural space to resource fails to let reality be. Instead, it hollows it out. Adapting the Thomistic principle *gratia non tollit naturam*, one could say that human creativity, properly practiced, enhances nature: *ars not tollit naturam, sed perficit*.

I will add one final remark about Heidegger's essay, regarding a point that is especially relevant in our theological context. The philosopher believes that the opening up of space that an authentic piece of architecture accomplishes cannot occur outside of a religious dimension. For someone familiar

115 Engelland, "Unmasking the Person," 459.

with the earlier Heidegger's attempts to distance himself from his religious roots—the protestations, in *Being and Time,* that notions like guilt or conscience are purely phenomenological—the following text is stunning:

> Always and ever differently the bridge guides the hesitant and hastening ways of men to and fro, so that they may get to other banks and in the end, as mortals, to the other side. Now in a high arch, now in a low, the bridge vaults over river and canyon—whether mortals keep in mind this vaulting of the bridge's course or forget that they, always themselves on their way to the last bridge, are at bottom striving to surmount all that is common and un-whole [*Unheiles*] in them in order to bring themselves before the wholeness [*das Heile*] of the divinities. The bridge *gathers,* as a vaulting passage, before the divinities—whether we explicitly

> think of, and visibly *give thanks for*, their presence, as in the figure of the saint of the bridge, or whether that divine presence is obstructed or even pushed aside.[116]

Heidegger is now really going too far, one might object, in projecting all this religious meaning onto the bridge. A bridge, after all, is just a bridge—in the American context, often a fairly crude piece of concrete stretching over a busy road. To which Heidegger would respond that such a bridge falls short of its essence. Such a bridge no longer speaks, and so fails to summon the humans crossing it to their finitude and the need for salvation.[117] Such a bridge contributes to a world in which we are no longer at home.

116 Heidegger, "Building Dwelling Thinking," 354–5/155. I have amended the translation significantly, both correcting mistakes (for instance, Heidegger's *Fluß und Schlucht*, "river and canyon," become "glen and stream" in the translation) and bringing out the etymological connection between *das Unheile* and *das Heile*.

117 *Heil* (without the final *e*) means "salvation."

Already attuned to a theological mode, we can now turn to Catholic space.

Catholic Space. Psalm 84, which I quoted earlier on, speaks of sparrows and swallows finding a home and a nest. The psalm views the human quest for a home mirrored in the animal world, and vice versa. Human beings do not live in an "environment" composed of "natural resources" but dwell in a shared world. Or, to put it differently, they exist as a microcosm embedded within the macrocosm.

Let us consider the fuller context of this verse. The beginning of Psalm 84 reads as follows:

1 How lovely is your dwelling place,
  Lord, God of hosts.
2 My soul is longing and yearning,
  is yearning for the courts of the Lord.
My heart and my soul ring out their joy
  to God, the living God.
3 The sparrow herself finds a home
  and the swallow a nest for her brood;
She lays her young by your altars,
  Lord of hosts, my king and my God.

4 They are happy, who dwell in your house,
for ever singing your praise.
They are happy, whose strength is in you,
in whose hearts are the roads to Sion.[118]

At the historical level, the psalm speaks of the experience of pilgrims in ancient Israel who were headed to Jerusalem. It gives expression to their longing to reach the sanctuary where the Lord dwells. Verse 4, "they are happy, who dwell in your house," may also be a reference to the cultic officials at work in the sanctuary. The psalm suggests that the Lord's house may be the ultimate dwelling place that human beings seek in their pilgrimage on earth. And, as we said, it likens the pilgrim's journey home to the nest-building of birds, thus placing the Book of Scripture alongside the Book of Nature, letting them illuminate each other.

Now let us read Psalm 84 in light of the following prayer, taken from the Liturgy of the Hours:

118 Quoted from the *Divine Office*, III, Week 3, Monday, Morning Prayer (pp. [284]–[285]).

> Father, the body of your risen Son is the temple not made by human hands and the defending wall of the new Jerusalem. May this holy city, built of living stones, shine with spiritual radiance and witness to your greatness in the sight of all nations.[119]

Once again, we find the typical figurative reading of the Old Covenant in light of the New. The physical Jerusalem with its temple has been transformed into a "new Jerusalem" that is spiritual, built of living stones—that is to say, people. These people are the faithful who are members of the Body of Christ. In one sense, they already live in the new Jerusalem, but in another sense, they are still awaiting its full realization.

A pilgrimage, then, is not an exceptional state, something in which devout people may choose to engage every now and then.

119 *The Divine Office*, vol. II: *Lenten Season, Easter Season* (New York: Catholic Book Publishing Corp., 1976), Week I, Thursday, Morning Prayer (p. 1166).

Rather, all of human life is a pilgrimage, all the time. The road to Sion is inscribed deep in our hearts. We are *in via*, as the Church used to say, "on the road." The Jewish people have always been, and in the Christian faith remain, the paradigm of a people in search of their home. The great Old Testament scholar Walter Brueggemann has gone so far as to suggest that "land is a central, if the not *the central theme* of biblical faith."[120] The story of God with his people in the Old Testament finds the Israelites almost constantly on the move, being called to their land, losing it, returning, losing it once again. This remains the story of the Jewish people until the present day, although that is, of course, no longer part of the Old Testament narrative.

Rome has not supplanted Jerusalem as

120 Walter Brueggemann, *The Land: Place as Gift, Promise, and Challenge in Biblical Faith* (London: SPCK, 1978), 187. John Inge builds on the work of Brueggemann (and others) in his *Christian Theology of Place*, Explorations in Practical, Pastoral, and Empirical Theology (Abingdon and New York: Routledge, 2016).

the spiritual center of Catholic space, since it is in Jerusalem that the drama of Jesus' story culminated in the events of Holy Week. At the same time, because the kingdom Jesus promised is not of this world, Jerusalem is now every place where the Body of Christ gathers, in particular to celebrate the Eucharist. Every church therefore is a small Jerusalem—and, indeed, with the liturgies of Palm Sunday and the Triduum of Holy Thursday, Good Friday, and the Easter Vigil this figure is re-enacted year after year. It is also worth pointing out that, while Jesus does not actually enter every church on Palm Sunday and does not suffer crucifixion again on Good Friday, in the Mass—every Mass—his sacrifice does become present.

Since every church is a new Jerusalem, the promised kingdom becomes present in it. This is why liturgical space and liturgical practice are as important as they are. In the space of a church, everything suggests redemption of the created order under the sign of the Cross. In his *Spirit of the Liturgy,* Ratzinger emphasizes one point specifically, with the greatest urgency: the cosmic dimension of Christian worship risks being lost if the rich symbolism of the sun is not upheld in the celebration *ad orientem*. He explains:

> Christians now face east, toward the rising sun. This is not a case of sun worship, but of the cosmos speaking of Christ. To him it is that the song of the sun in Psalm 19(18) is now applied. There it says: "It (the sun) comes forth like a bridegroom coming from his tent. . . . At the end of the sky is the rising of the sun; to the furthest end of the sky is its course" (verses 6–7). . . . Christians interpret [the psalm] in terms of Christ, who is the living Word, the eternal Logos, and thus the true light of history, who came forth in Bethlehem from the bridal chamber of the Virgin Mother and now illuminates the entire world.[121]

Here we see again the complex interplay that

is at the heart of Christian language as it sublates the cosmic order into salvation history, and the Old Testament into the New. And again, it is appropriate to call to mind the Thomistic principle, *gratia non tollit naturam, sed perficit*. To be sure, the Christian liturgy is not a case of sun worship, but neither is the natural order left behind. It is, as Thomas says, "perfected," taken up into the order of grace.

This perfection of nature through grace extends to every aspect of the liturgy, beyond the spatial orientation of the celebration. Voices no longer merely speak, but break into songs of praise. Light does not shine directly, blinding us, but is refracted through stained glass windows which let it tell its story as God's first creation. The sense of

121 Ratzinger, *Theology of the Liturgy*, 41/73. I have revised the translation, using the version from the Divine Office for the psalm. For more detailed discussion of celebration *ad orientem*, see Uwe Michael Lang, *Turning Towards the Lord: Orientation in Liturgical Prayer* (San Francisco: Ignatius Press, 2009). The book carries a foreword by then Joseph Cardinal Ratzinger.

smell is elevated as incense is burnt, one of the most ancient objects of sacrifice. The food supplied at Mass is simultaneously bread, manna from heaven, and the Body of Christ. All of this occurs in the medium of language, which holds the figurative meanings together and performs the transubstantiation of a liturgical space here on earth into an instance of the new Jerusalem.

Let us break off here. What has been offered up to this point is a mere sketch. In a more comprehensive account of Catholic space, one would have to discuss holy places that exist outside of churches (such as holy wells and shrines), pilgrimages, processions, and the like—all symbols of the new Jerusalem and of the paths thereto.

IV

Conclusion

This lecture opened with the discussion of a paradox that is tearing at the seams of contemporary Western society. Human beings are widely believed to be endowed with the right—indeed, the fundamental human right—to constitute their identities in a radically autonomous manner, even when such self-constitution involves supposed biological givens like sex. In certain contexts, however, such autonomous self-constitution is excluded, as in matters of race. Both convictions are held with equal passion and vehemence, often by the same people. Since both aspects of this social and political controversy concern the biological sphere, we are dealing with an instance of what Foucault has termed "biopolitics."

The roots of this biopolitical paradox run deep, to the anthropology of the empirico-transcendental doublet in which, according to Foucault, modern thought has been caught up since Kant. To address the tension requires the ability to think the human being at once, and without contradiction, as subject in both senses of the term, active and passive—that is to say, as both constitutive subject and subject *to* constitution. It requires, as Foucault puts it, a mode of thought in which it is possible to think together the being of man and the being of language. It requires, in different yet still Foucauldian terms, technologies of the self which articulate strategies for self-governance in the face of overwhelming powers of normalization.

To discover such technologies of the self, Foucault embarked upon serious study of the Church Fathers. In this lecture, I have attempted to take up and deepen Foucault's groundbreaking research by sketching the outlines of the "liturgical subject." I have done so guided by the liturgical theology of Joseph Ratzinger, in a move that has brought into dialogue one of the most influential philosophers of the twentieth century with an equally towering figure in Catholic theology. The juxtaposition might appear jarring to some, but it has produced fruitful insights.

Speaking of a liturgical subject implies agreement with the Kantian claim that the reality in which we live is humanly constituted. There is no world-in-itself accessible to the human mind,[122] no natural world that is not already cultural—and this, *pace* Kant, also means that there is no human world that is not historical. The liturgical subject differs

122 It is worth pointing out that this seemingly radical claim corresponds to a time-honored insight into the limitations of the human intellect's ability to grasp the essences of things. Consider the following passages from two works of St. Thomas Aquinas: (1) *In symbolum Apostolorum,* prologus, § 864: "cognitio nostra est adeo debilis quod nullus philosophus potuit unquam perfecte investigare naturam unius muscae: unde legitur, quod unus philosophus fuit triginta annis in solitudine, ut cognosceret naturam apis"; (2) *De ente et essentia,* chap. 5 (Ed. leon. XLIII: 379): "In rebus enim sensibilibus etiam ipse differentie essentiales ignote sunt; unde significantur per differentias accidentales que ex essentialibus oriuntur, sicut causa significatur per suum effectum, sicut bipes ponitur differentia hominis."

radically from the modern one, however, in that its constitution of self and world is not autonomous but occurs, rather, in response to a preceding, more fundamental initiative—namely, God's creative and redemptive action. Indeed, in Christian terms, self-constitution outside of or against God's prior constitution is the philosophical meaning of sin.

In the liturgical context, self-constitution occurs through the putting on of Christ, symbolized paradigmatically in the liturgical vestments in which the priest clothes himself for the celebration of the Eucharist. Such *Christuswerden*, becoming Christ, is possible only because Christ first put on humanity and, in the Eucharistic celebration, even deigns to put on the appearance of lowly bread and wine. Furthermore, at the crucial moment when the words of consecration are uttered, the priest cedes the initiative to God, speaking *in persona Christi*. Role play must become reality so that the performative speech act may be successful.

The Christian life has its center on that stage where Mass is performed, but the performance radiates out into all parts of reality, permeating it with grace. In this process, even the basic dimensions of time and space put on Christ, acquiring a Christian structure. Thus elevated in liturgical action and speech, the created order is sanctified, that is to say, explicitly ordered toward the Creator from whom it originated. In this way, *gratia perficit naturam*: it is through grace that nature comes to its *telos* and perfection, whereas outside of grace, cut off from God's redemptive influence, the created order stands at risk of being reduced to mere resource, along with man himself. The liturgical subject functions as a conduit of grace, such that even *ars non tollit naturam, sed perficit*. Where human art subverts nature, on the other hand, catastrophe will ensue. Considered in this perspective, our current ecological crisis is the manifestation of sin. It is no coincidence that in the Old Testament, and the Psalms in particular, human disobedience regularly triggers cosmic consequences. Only once the relationship between God and man is healed can there be a return to a healthy relationship with the created order more generally.

The possibility of such a return hinges on our ability to relearn figurative language, language that lets things speak and reconnects us with a cosmos that carries meaning. It is figurative language, moreover, which renders the fulfillment of the Old Covenant by the New intelligible, the dynamism on which the Christian faith turns. It is a matter of great concern, therefore, that our contemporary Western culture suffers from univocity: language is serious, scientific, reductive—and increasingly fanatical as well. But a mountain that is nothing more than a mountain falls silent. It risks becoming resource, for economic purposes like mining or the tourism industry. It becomes impossible to experience it as a fellow creature that wants to tell us something. What could its message be? There were people before us who still had the ears to hear and eyes to read the Book of Nature, people like the prophet Daniel, who composed a beautiful hymn in which he imagined all of creation glorifying the Creator. The Church still recites this hymn regularly in her Liturgy of the Hours, where it features in the morning prayer (Lauds) on Sundays, solemnities, and feasts. We close with a brief excerpt (Dan. 3:75–77):

And you, mountains and hills, O bless the
Lord.
And you, all plants of the earth, O bless the
Lord.
And you, fountains and springs, O bless the
Lord.
To him be highest glory and praise for
ever.[123]

123 Quoted from *The Divine Office: The Liturgy of the Hours according to the Roman Rite*, vol. I, Christmas Day, Morning Prayer, p. 190.